# React Application Architecture for Production

Learn best practices and expert tips to deliver enterprise-ready React web apps

**Alan Alickovic**

BIRMINGHAM—MUMBAI

# React Application Architecture for Production

**Group Product Manager**: Pavan Ramchandani
**Publishing Product Manager**: Aaron Tanna
**Senior Editor**: Aamir Ahmed
**Content Development Editor**: Abhishek Jadhav
**Technical Editor**: Simran Udasi
**Copy Editor**: Safis Editing
**Project Coordinator**: Aishwarya Mohan
**Proofreader**: Safis Editing
**Indexer**: Rekha Nair
**Production Designer**: Vijay Kamble
**Marketing Coordinator**: Anamika Singh

First published: December 2022

Production reference: 1011222

Published by Packt Publishing Ltd.
Livery Place
35 Livery Street
Birmingham
B3 2PB, UK.

ISBN 978-1-80107-053-9

www.packt.com

*To my younger self.*

*– Alan Alickovic*

# Contributors

## About the author

**Alan Alickovic** is a software engineer, consultant, mentor, and open source enthusiast. During the years of his software engineering career, he has gained extensive experience in building applications of various scales for start-ups and large organizations in a variety of different industries. He also has plenty of experience in leading and mentoring engineers and helping them grow and progress in their careers.

*A huge thanks to the awesome Packt team that worked with me on this book. Their support and guidance throughout the entire process were the key components in making this book possible.*

*A big thanks to all the reviewers that made an effort to go over the book and point out things that could be improved.*

*I would also like to thank all my awesome colleagues and the people I have worked with throughout my career, for the valuable lessons I learned from them and for making my job easier.*

*And finally, special thanks goes to my family and friends, for their unconditional patience and support.*

# About the reviewers

**Pawel Czekaj** has a bachelor's degree in computer science. He has 12 years of experience as a frontend developer. Currently, he works as a principal software engineer at Ziflow Ltd. He has expertise in Angular, React.js, Amazon Web Services, Auth0, NestJS, and many other frameworks. He is currently working on enterprise-level proofing solutions built with Angular and Spring Boot.

**Kirill Ezhemenskii** is an experienced software engineer, a frontend and mobile developer, a solution architect, and the CTO at a healthcare company. He's a functional programming advocate and an expert in the React stack, GraphQL and TypeScript. He's also a React Native mentor.

# Table of Contents

# 6

# Integrating the API into the Application                                    105

# 7

# Implementing User Authentication and Global Notifications                   125

# 8

# Testing                                                                     145

# 9

## Configuring CI/CD for Testing and Deployment                        171

# 10

## Going Beyond                                                          187

## Index                                                                 203

## Other Books You May Enjoy                                             210

# Preface

Building large-scale applications in production with React can be overwhelming with the number of choices and lack of cohesive resources. This hands-on guide is designed to share practices and examples to help address these challenges in building enterprise-ready applications with React.

This book provides a concrete and practical example, developed throughout, to demonstrate the concepts in the book. You will learn how to build modern frontend applications from scratch that are ready for production. Beginning with getting an overview of the React ecosystem, you will identify the tools available to solve complex development challenges. You will learn how to build mocked APIs, components, and pages that form a complete frontend app. The book will also share practices for testing, securing, and packaging your app in a structured way. Finally, you will learn how to deploy your app to production with scalability in mind.

By the end of the book, you will be able to efficiently build production-ready applications by following industry practices and expert tips.

## Who this book is for

This book is for intermediate-level web developers that already have a good understanding of JavaScript, React, and web development in general and want to build large-scale React applications effectively. Besides experience with JavaScript and React, some experience with TypeScript will be beneficial.

## What this book covers

*Chapter 1*, *Understanding the Architecture of React Applications*, teaches you how to think about applications from an architectural point of view. It starts by covering the importance of good architecture and its benefits. Then, it covers some bad and good practices in React applications. Finally, we will cover the planning of a real React application, which we will be building throughout the book.

*Chapter 2*, *Setup and Project Structure Overview*, covers all the tools and setup for the application that we will be building. It will introduce us to tools such as Next.js, TypeScript, ESLint, Prettier, Husky, and Lint Staged. Finally, it will cover the feature-based project structure for the project, which improves the code base organization.

*Chapter 3*, *Building and Documenting Components*, introduces us to Chakra UI, a great component library that we will be using as building blocks for our UI. We will cover setting it up, and then we will build the components that we can reuse all over the application to make the UI of the application more consistent. Finally, we will learn about documenting those components with Storybook.

*Chapter 4, Building and Configuring Pages,* covers Next.js in more depth. First, we will cover the basics, such as Next.js routing and the rendering strategies it supports. Then, we will learn how to handle shared layouts. Finally, we will apply those techniques by building the pages for our application.

*Chapter 5, Mocking the API,* dives deep into mocking the API that can be used for development and testing. It starts by explaining why it is useful. Then, it introduces the MSW library, which allows mocking API endpoints in an elegant way. Finally, we will apply what we have learned by implementing the endpoints for our application.

*Chapter 6, Integrating the API into the Application,* teaches us how to communicate with the backend API. We will learn how to configure the API client and React Query and use that to build the API layer for our application. Then, we will apply what we have learned by implementing the API calls for our application.

*Chapter 7, Implementing User Authentication and Global Notifications,* starts by teaching you how to implement the authentication for your application. Then, it demonstrates how to handle the global state by implementing the notifications system for our application.

*Chapter 8, Testing,* teaches you how to approach testing a React application. It covers unit testing with Jest, integration testing with Jest and React Testing Library, and end-to-end testing with Cypress.

*Chapter 9, Configuring CI/CD for Testing and Deployment,* covers the basics of a GitHub Actions pipeline. Then, we will learn how to configure the pipeline for code checking and testing. Finally, we will configure it for deployment to Vercel.

*Chapter 10, Going Beyond,* touches on some uncovered topics. Since the application is at the MVP stage, there is room for improvement, and this chapter covers some of those improvements. We will also learn about some technical improvements that would help the application scale even further.

## To get the most out of this book

Previous experience with JavaScript and React and fundamental knowledge of web development will make it a lot easier to follow along with the content of the book. It is also desirable to have some experience with TypeScript and Next.js, but it should be possible to follow along without it since we will cover the basics in the book.

| Software/hardware covered in the book | Operating system requirements |
| --- | --- |
| React 18 | macOS, Windows, or Linux |
| Next.js 12 | |
| TypeScript 4.8 | |

If you are using the digital version of this book, we advise you to type the code yourself or access the code from the book's GitHub repository (a link is available in the next section). Doing so will help you avoid any potential errors related to the copying and pasting of code.

For more details and information about the setup and requirements, it is best to check the README file in the book's GitHub repository.

## Download the example code files

You can download the example code files for this book from GitHub at `https://github.com/PacktPublishing/React-Application-Architecture-for-Production`. If there's an update to the code, it will be updated in the GitHub repository.

We also have other code bundles from our rich catalog of books and videos available at `https://github.com/PacktPublishing/`. Check them out!

## Download the color images

We also provide a PDF file that has color images of the screenshots and diagrams used in this book. You can download it here: `https://packt.link/DjfrW`.

## Conventions used

There are a number of text conventions used throughout this book.

`Code in text`: Indicates code words in text, database table names, folder names, filenames, file extensions, pathnames, dummy URLs, user input, and Twitter handles. Here is an example: "Let's create the `.github/workflows/main.yml` file and the initial code."

A block of code is set as follows:

```
name: CI/CD
on:
  - push
jobs:
# add jobs here
```

When we wish to draw your attention to a particular part of a code block, the relevant lines or items are set in bold:

```
jobs:
  # previous jobs
  e2e:
```

```
name: E2E Tests
runs-on: ubuntu-latest
steps:
  - uses: actions/checkout@v3
  - run: mv .env.example .env
  - uses: cypress-io/github-action@v4
    with:
        build: npm run build
        start: npm run start
```

Any command-line input or output is written as follows:

```
git clone https://github.com/PacktPublishing/React-Application-
Architecture-for-Production.git
```

**Bold**: Indicates a new term, an important word, or words that you see on screen. For instance, words in menus or dialog boxes appear in **bold**. Here is an example: "When the user clicks the **Apply** button, the email client is opened with the correctly set subject."

> **Tips or important notes**
> Appear like this.

## Get in touch

Feedback from our readers is always welcome.

**General feedback**: If you have questions about any aspect of this book, email us at customercare@ packtpub.com and mention the book title in the subject of your message.

**Errata**: Although we have taken every care to ensure the accuracy of our content, mistakes do happen. If you have found a mistake in this book, we would be grateful if you would report this to us. Please visit www.packtpub.com/support/errata and fill in the form.

**Piracy**: If you come across any illegal copies of our works in any form on the internet, we would be grateful if you would provide us with the location address or website name. Please contact us at copyright@packt.com with a link to the material.

**If you are interested in becoming an author**: If there is a topic that you have expertise in and you are interested in either writing or contributing to a book, please visit authors.packtpub.com.

## Share Your Thoughts

Once you've read *React Application Architecture for Production*, we'd love to hear your thoughts! Scan the QR code below to go straight to the Amazon review page for this book and share your feedback.

https://www.amazon.in/review/create-review/error?asin=1801070539

Your review is important to us and the tech community and will help us make sure we're delivering excellent quality content.

# Download a free PDF copy of this book

Thanks for purchasing this book!

Do you like to read on the go but are unable to carry your print books everywhere?

Is your eBook purchase not compatible with the device of your choice?

Don't worry, now with every Packt book you get a DRM-free PDF version of that book at no cost.

Read anywhere, any place, on any device. Search, copy, and paste code from your favorite technical books directly into your application.

The perks don't stop there, you can get exclusive access to discounts, newsletters, and great free content in your inbox daily

Follow these simple steps to get the benefits:

1.  Scan the QR code or visit the link below

https://packt.link/free-ebook/9781801070539

2.  Submit your proof of purchase

3.  That's it! We'll send your free PDF and other benefits to your email directly

# Understanding the Architecture of React Applications

React is an open source JavaScript library for building user interfaces created and maintained by Meta (Facebook).

It is probably the most popular library for building user interfaces nowadays. The reason for its popularity is that it is quite performant and has a small API, which makes it a simple yet very powerful tool for creating user interfaces.

It is component-based, which allows us to split large applications into smaller parts and work on them in isolation.

React is also great because its core API is decoupled from the platform, allowing projects such as React Native to exist outside the web platform.

One of React's biggest strengths but also weaknesses is that it is very flexible. This has allowed its community to build great solutions. However, defining a good application architecture out of the box can be challenging.

Making the right architectural decisions is crucial for any application to succeed, especially once it needs changes or it grows in terms of size, the number of users, and the number of people working on it.

In this chapter, we will cover the following topics:

- Benefits of having a good application architecture
- Exploring the architectural challenges of React applications
- Understanding architectural decisions when building React applications
- Planning our application

By the end of this chapter, we will learn to think a bit more from the architectural point of view when starting React application development.

# Benefits of having a good application architecture

Every application uses some architecture, even without thinking about it. It might have been chosen randomly and might not be the right one for its needs and requirements, but still, every application does have an architecture.

That's why being mindful of the proper architecture at the beginning is essential for every project. Let's define a couple of reasons why:

- A good foundation for the project
- Easier project management
- Increased development speed and productivity
- Cost-effectiveness
- Better product quality

It is worth noting that all applications are prone to requirement changes, so it is not always possible to predict everything upfront. However, we should be mindful of the architecture from the start. We will discuss these reasons in detail in the following sections.

## A good foundation for the project

Every building should be built on solid foundations to remain resilient to different conditions such as age, weather conditions, earthquakes, and other causes.

The same thing can apply to applications. Multiple factors cause various changes during a project's lifetime, such as changes in requirements, organization, technologies, market, finance, and more. Being built on solid foundations will make it resilient to all those changes.

## Easier project management

Having different components organized properly will make organizing and delegating tasks much easier, especially if a larger team is involved.

Good component decoupling will allow better splitting of work between teams and team members and faster iterations without team members being blocked by each other.

It also allows better estimates to be made regarding how much time is required for a feature to be completed.

## Increased development speed and productivity

Having a good architecture defined allows developers to focus on the product they are building without overthinking the technical implementations since most of the technical decisions should have already been made.

Besides that, it will provide a smoother onboarding process for new developers, who can be productive quickly after familiarizing themselves with the overall architecture.

## Cost-effectiveness

All the reasons mentioned in the previous sections indicate that the improvements a good architecture brings will reduce costs.

In most cases, the most expensive cost of every project is people and their work and time. Therefore, by allowing them to be more efficient, we can reduce some redundant costs a bad architecture could bring.

It will also allow better financial analysis and planning of pricing models for software products. It will make it easier to predict all the costs the platform requires to be functional.

## Better product quality

Making all team members productive gives them time to focus and spend more time on important things, such as the business requirements and the needs of users, rather than spending most of the time fixing bugs and reducing technical debt.

Better product quality will also make our users more satisfied, which should be the end goal.

To exist, every piece of software needs to meet its requirements. We'll see what these software requirements are in the following section.

# Exploring the architectural challenges of React applications

In this section, we will focus on React and see what things are necessary to consider when building React applications and the main challenges most React developers face when building their applications.

## What are the challenges when building a React application?

React is a great tool for building user interfaces. However, there are some challenging things we should think about when building an application. It is very flexible, which is both a good and a bad thing. It is good in the sense that we can define the architecture of different parts of the application without the library getting in our way.

By being so flexible, React has gathered a large community of developers worldwide, building different open-source solutions. There is a complete solution for literally any problem we might encounter during development. This makes the React ecosystem very rich.

However, that flexibility and ecosystem richness come with a cost.

Let's take a look at the following React ecosystem overview diagram made by `roadmap.sh`:

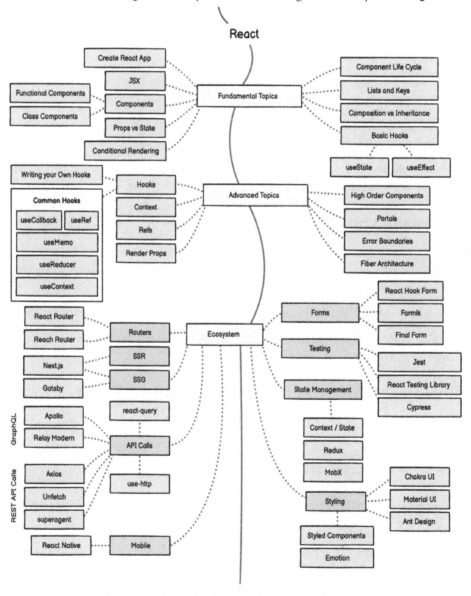

Figure 1.1 – React developer roadmap by roadmap.sh

As shown in *Figure 1.1*, there is a lot to consider when building an application with React. Let's also keep in mind that this diagram might show just the tip of the iceberg. Many different packages and solutions could be used to build the same application.

Some of the most frequent questions when starting with a new React application are as follows:

- What project structure are we using?
- What rendering strategy are we using?
- What state management solution are we using?
- What styling solution are we using?
- What data fetching approach are we using?
- How are we going to handle user authentication?
- What testing strategies are we going to use?

These challenges are not limited to React – they are relevant to building frontend applications in general, regardless of which tools are being used. But since this book focuses on React, we will be approaching them from that perspective.

## What project structure are we using?

Because React is very flexible and has a very small API, it is unopinionated about how we should structure our projects. Here is what *Dan Abramov*, one of the maintainers of React, says on this:

*"Move files around until it feels right"*

And that is a very good point. It will mostly depend on the nature of the application. For example, we wouldn't organize a social network application and a text editor application in the same way because they have different needs and different problems to solve.

## What rendering strategy are we using?

It depends on the nature of our application.

If we are building an internal dashboard application, a single-page application is more than enough.

On the other hand, if we build a customer-facing application that should also be public and SEO-friendly, we should think about server-side rendering or static generation, depending on how often the data on the pages are being updated.

## What state management solution are we using?

React comes with built-in state management mechanisms with its hooks and Context API, but for more complex applications, we often reach for external solutions such as **Redux**, **MobX**, **Zustand**, **Recoil**, and others.

Choosing the right state management solution is something that depends a lot on the application's needs and requirements. We will not reach for the same tools if we are building a to-do app or an e-commerce application.

It mostly depends on the amount of state that needs to be shared across the entire application and the frequency of updating those pieces of state.

Will our application have a lot of frequent updates? If that is the case, we might consider atom-based solutions such as **Recoil** or **Jotai**.

If our application requires a lot of different components to share the same state, then **Redux** with **Redux Toolkit** is a good option.

On the other hand, if we do not have a lot of global states and don't update it very often, then **Zustand** or **React Context API**, in combination with hooks, are good choices.

At the end of the day, it all depends on the application's needs and the nature of the problem we are trying to solve.

## What styling solution are we using?

This one mostly depends on preference. Some people prefer vanilla CSS, some people love utility-first CSS libraries such as **Tailwind**, and some developers can't live without **CSS in JS**.

Making this decision should also depend on whether our application will be re-rendered very often. If that is the case, we might consider build-time solutions such as vanilla CSS, SCSS, Tailwind, and others. Otherwise, we can use runtime styling solutions such as **Styled Components**, **Emotion**, and more.

We should also keep in mind whether we want to use a pre-built component library or if we want to build everything from scratch.

## How are we going to handle user authentication?

This depends on the API implementation. Are we using token-based authentication? Does our API server support cookie-based authentication? It is considered to be safer to use cookie-based authentication with `httpOnly` cookies to prevent **cross-site scripting** (**XSS**) attacks.

Most of these things should be defined together with the backend teams.

### What testing strategies are we going to use?

This depends on the team structure, so if we have QA engineers available, we will be able to let them do end-to-end tests.

It also depends on how much time we can devote to testing and other aspects. Keep in mind that we should always consider having some level of testing, at least integration, and end-to-end testing for the most critical parts of our application.

# Understanding architectural decisions when building React applications

Regardless of the specific needs of the application, there are some generally bad and good decisions we can make when building it.

## Bad architectural decisions

Let's look at some of the bad architectural decisions that might slow us down.

### Flat project structure

Imagine having a lot of components, all living in the same folder. The simplest thing to do is to place all the React components within the components folder, which is fine if our components count does not exceed 20 components. After that, it becomes difficult to find where a component should belong because they are all mixed.

### Large, tightly coupled components

Having large and coupled components have a couple of downsides. They are difficult to test in isolation, they are difficult to reuse, and they may also have performance issues in some cases because the component would need to be re-rendered entirely instead of us re-rendering just a small part of it that needs to be re-rendered.

### Unnecessary global state

Having a global state is fine, and often required. But keeping too many things in a global state can be a bad idea. It might affect performance, but also maintainability because it makes it difficult to understand the scope of the state.

### Using the wrong tools to solve problems

The number of choices in the React ecosystem makes it easier to choose the wrong tools to solve a problem – for example, caching server responses in the global store. It may be possible, and we have been doing this in the past, but that doesn't mean we should keep doing that because there are tools to solve this problem, such as React Query, SWR, Apollo Client, and so on.

### Putting the entire application in a single component in a single file

This is something that shouldn't ever happen, but it is still worth mentioning. Nothing is preventing us from creating a complete application in a single file. It could be thousands of lines long – that is, a single component that would do everything. But for the same reason as having large components, it should be avoided.

### Not sanitizing user inputs

Many hackers on the web are trying to steal our user's data. Therefore, we should do everything possible to prevent such things from happening. By sanitizing user inputs, we can prevent hackers from executing some malicious piece of code in our application and stealing user data. For example, we should prevent our users from inputting anything that could be executed in our application by removing any parts of the input that might be risky.

### Using unoptimized infrastructure to serve our application

Using unoptimized infrastructure to serve our application will make our application slow when accessed from different parts of the world.

Now that we have covered some bad architectural decisions, let's see how to improve them.

## Good architectural decisions

Let's look at some of the good decisions we can make to make our application better.

### Better structured project structure based on domain and features

Splitting the application structure into different features or domain-specific modules, each responsible for its own role, will allow better separation of concerns of different application pieces, better modularity of different parts of the application, better flexibility, and scalability.

### Better state management

Instead of putting everything in a global state, we should start by defining a piece of a state as close as possible to where it is being used in the component and lift it only if necessary.

### Smaller components

Having smaller components will make them more testable, easier to track changes, and easier to work in larger teams.

### *Separation of concerns*

Have each component do as little as possible. This makes components easy to understand, test, modify, and even reuse.

### *Static code analysis*

Relying on static code analysis tools such as **ESLint**, **Prettier**, and **TypeScript** will improve our code quality without us having to think too much about it. We just need to configure these tools, and they will let us know when something is wrong with our code. These tools also introduce consistency in the code base regarding formatting, code practices, and documentation.

### *Deploying the application over a CDN*

Having users worldwide means our application should be functional and accessible from all over the world. By deploying the application on a CDN, users all over the world can access the application in the most optimal way.

# Planning our application

Now, let's apply the principles we just learned about to a real-world scenario where we will be planning the application that we will be building.

## What are we building?

We will be building an application that allows organizations to manage their job boards. The organization admins can create job postings for their organizations, and the candidates can apply for the jobs.

We will be building an MVP version of the application with the minimum set of features, but it should be extendable for more features in the future. At the end of this book, we will cover the features that the final application could have, but to keep things simple, we will be focusing on the MVP version.

Proper application planning starts with gathering the requirements of the application.

## Application requirements

The application has two types of application requirements:

- Functional requirements
- Non-functional requirements

## *Functional requirements*

Functional requirements should define what the application should do. They are descriptions of all the features and functionalities of an application that our users would use.

Our application can be split into two parts:

- Publicly facing part
- Organization admin dashboard

### Publicly facing part

- Landing page with some basic information about our application.
- Public organization view where the visitors can find information about the given organization. Besides the basic organization information, it should also include the list of jobs of the organization.
- A public job view where the visitors can view some basic information about the given job. Besides this information, it should also include the action for applying for the job.

### Organization admin dashboard

- Authentication system for the dashboard that should allow organization admins to authenticate into the dashboard. For our MVP, we will just implement the login functionality with an existing test user.
- Jobs list view where the admin can view all the jobs of the organization.
- Create a job view that contains the form for creating new jobs.
- Job details view, which contains all the information about the job.

## *Non-functional requirements*

Non-functional requirements should define how the application should work from the technical side:

- **Performance**: The application must be interactive within 5 seconds. By that, we mean that the user should be able to interact with the page within 5 seconds from when the request to load the application was made until the user can interact with the page.
- **Usability**: The application must be user-friendly and intuitive. This includes implementing responsive design for smaller screens. We want the user experience to be smooth and straightforward.
- **SEO**: The public-facing pages of the application should be SEO-friendly.

# Data model overview

To better understand how our application will work under the hood, it is helpful to understand its data model, so we will dive into that in this section.

In the following diagram, we can see what our data model looks like from the database perspective:

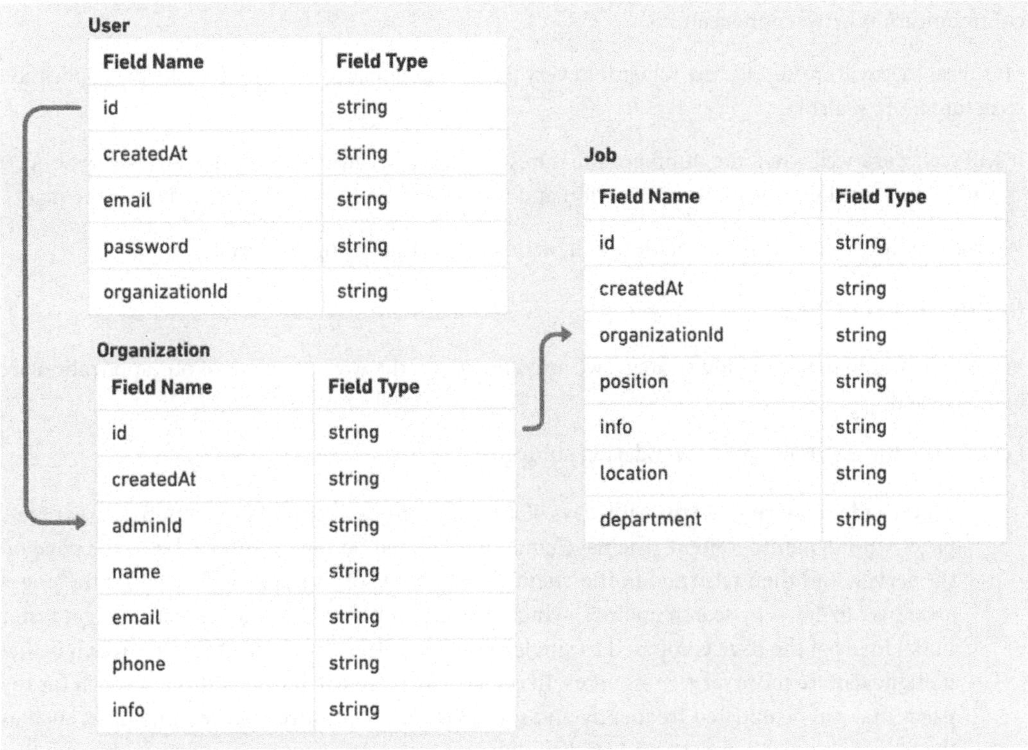

**User**

| Field Name | Field Type |
|---|---|
| id | string |
| createdAt | string |
| email | string |
| password | string |
| organizationId | string |

**Job**

| Field Name | Field Type |
|---|---|
| id | string |
| createdAt | string |
| organizationId | string |
| position | string |
| info | string |
| location | string |
| department | string |

**Organization**

| Field Name | Field Type |
|---|---|
| id | string |
| createdAt | string |
| adminId | string |
| name | string |
| email | string |
| phone | string |
| info | string |

Figure 1.2 – Data model overview

As seen in *Figure 1.2*, there are three main models in the application:

- User
- Organization
- Job

Defining the application requirements and data model should give us a good understanding of what we are building. Now, let's explore the technical decisions for our application.

## Exploring the technical decisions

Let's see what technical decisions we need to make for our application.

### *Project structure*

We will be using a feature-based project structure that allows good feature isolation and good communication between the features.

This means we will create a feature folder for every larger functionality, which will make the application structure more scalable.

It will scale very well when the number of features increases because we only need to worry about a specific feature and not the entire application at once, where the code is scattered all over the place.

We will see the project structure definition in action in the upcoming chapters.

### *Rendering strategy*

When it comes to the rendering strategy, we are referring to the way the pages of our application are being created.

Let's look at the different types of rendering strategies:

- **Server-side rendering**: In the early days of the web, this was the most common way to generate pages with dynamic content. The page content is created on the fly, inserted into the page on the server, and then returned to the client. The benefits of this approach are that the pages are easier to crawl by search engines, which is important for SEO, and users might get faster initial loads of the page compared to single-page apps. The downside of this approach is that it might require more server resources. In our scenario, we will be using this approach for the pages that can be updated frequently and should be SEO optimized at the same time, such as the public organization page and public job page.

- **Client-side rendering**: The existence of client-side JavaScript libraries and frameworks, such as React, Angular, Vue, and others, allows us to create complex client-side applications completely on the client. The benefit of this is that once the application is loaded in the browser, the transition between pages seems very fast. On the other hand, for the application to load, we need to download a lot of JavaScript to use the application. This can be improved by code splitting and lazy loading. It is also more difficult to crawl the page's content using search engines, which can impact SEO scores. We can use this approach for protected pages, which is every page in the dashboard of our application.

- **Static generation**: This is the most straightforward approach. Here, we can generate our pages while building the application and serve them statically. It is very fast, and we can use this approach for pages that never update but need to be SEO optimized, such as the landing page of our application.

Since our application requires multiple rendering strategies, we will use Next.js, which supports each of them very well.

## State management

State management is probably one of the most discussed topics in the React ecosystem. It is very fragmented, meaning there are so many libraries that handle state that it makes it difficult for the developers to make a choice.

To make state management easier for us, we need to understand that there are multiple types of states:

- **Local state**: This is the simplest type of state. It is the state that is being used in a single component only and is not required anywhere else. We will use the built-in React hooks to handle that.

- **Global state**: This is the state that is shared across multiple components in the application. It is used to avoid prop drilling. We will be using a lightweight library called **Zustand** for this.

- **Server state**: This state is used to store data responses from the API. Things such as loading states, request de-duplications, polling, and others are very challenging to implement from scratch. Therefore, we will be using **React Query** to handle this elegantly so that we have less code to write.

- **Form state**: This should handle form inputs, validation, and other aspects. We will be using the **React Hook Form** library to handle forms in our application.

- **URL state**: This type of state is often overlooked yet very powerful. URL and query params can also be considered as pieces of state. This is especially useful when we want to deep-link some part of the view. Capturing the state in the URL makes it very easy to share it.

## Styling

Styling is also a big topic in the React ecosystem. There are many great libraries for styling React components.

To style our application, we will use the **Chakra UI** component library, which uses Emotion under the hood, and it comes with a variety of nice-looking and accessible components that are very flexible and easy to modify.

The reason for choosing Chakra UI is that it has a great developer experience. It is very customizable, and its components are accessibility-friendly out of the box.

## Authentication

The authentication of our application will be cookie-based, meaning that on a successful auth request, a cookie will be attached to the headers, which will handle user authentication on the server. We are choosing cookie-based authentication because it is more secure.

## *Testing*

Testing is a very important method of asserting that our application is working as it's supposed to.

We don't want to ship our product with bugs in it. Also, manual testing takes more time and effort to discover new bugs, so we want to have automated tests for our application.

There are multiple types of tests:

- **Unit tests**: Unit tests only test the smallest units of an application in isolation. We will be using **Jest** to unit-test the shared components of our application.

- **Integration tests**: Integration tests test multiple units at once. They are very useful for testing the communication between multiple different parts of the application. We will be using **React Testing Library** to test our pages.

- **End-to-end tests**: End-to-end tests allow us to test our application's most important parts end to end, meaning we can test the entire flow. Usually, the most important end-to-end tests should test the most critical features. For this kind of testing, we will be using **Cypress**.

This was an overview of how our application should work. Now, we should be able to start implementing it in code in the upcoming chapters.

## Summary

React is a very popular library for building user interfaces, and it leaves most of the architectural choices to developers, which can be challenging.

In this chapter, we learned that some of the benefits of setting up a good architecture are a good project foundation, easier project management, increased productivity, cost-effectiveness, and better product quality.

We also learned about the challenges to consider, such as project structure, rendering strategies, state management, styling, authentication, testing, and others.

Then, we covered the planning phase of the application that we will be building, which is an application for managing job boards and job applications by gathering requirements. We did that by defining the data model of the application and choosing the right tools to overcome the architectural challenges.

This has given us a good foundation to implement our architecture in a real-world scenario, as we will see in the following chapters.

In the next chapter, we will cover the entire setup that we will be using for building the application.

# 2
# Setup and Project Structure Overview

In the previous chapter, we looked at all the challenges when building a React application and some great solutions that can help us handle them. We also planned out how our application should work and what tools we should use.

In this chapter, we will look at the project structure and the setup tools that make a good baseline for our project.

We will cover the following topics:

- Next.js application overview
- TypeScript setup overview and usage
- ESLint setup overview
- Prettier setup overview
- Pre-committing checks setup overview
- Project structure overview

By the end of this chapter, we will have a good understanding of the tools we will be using for the project setup and the feature-based project structure to make organizing our code more manageable.

# Technical requirements

Before we get started, we need to set up our project. To be able to develop our project, we will need the following things installed on our computer:

- **Node.js** version 16 or above and **npm** version 8 or above.

  There are multiple ways to install Node.js and npm. Here is a great article that goes into more detail: `https://www.nodejsdesignpatterns.com/blog/5-ways-to-install-node-js`.

- **VSCode** (optional) is currently the most popular editor/IDE for JavaScript/TypeScript, so we will be using it. It is open source, has great integration with TypeScript, and we can extend its features via extensions. It can be downloaded from `https://code.visualstudio.com/`.

The code files for this chapter can be found here: `https://github.com/PacktPublishing/React-Application-Architecture-for-Production`.

The repository can be cloned locally with the following command:

```
git clone https://github.com/PacktPublishing/React-Application-
Architecture-for-Production.git
```

Once the repository has been cloned, we need to install the application's dependencies:

```
npm install
```

We also need to provide the environment variables:

```
cp .env.example .env
```

Once the dependencies have been installed, we need to select the right stage of the code base that matches this chapter. We can do that by executing the following command:

```
npm run stage:switch
```

This command will prompt us with a list of stages for each chapter:

```
? What stage do you want to switch to? (Use arrow
  keys)
> chapter-02
  chapter-03
  chapter-03-start
  chapter-04
  chapter-04-start
```

```
    chapter-05
    chapter-05-start
  (Move up and down to reveal more choices)
```

This is the second chapter so we can select the chapter-02 option.

Once the chapter has been selected, all files required to follow along with the chapter will appear. To follow along with this chapter, we don't need to make any changes to the code. We can just use it as a reference to help get a better overview of the code base.

For more information about the setup details, check out the README.md file.

# Next.js application overview

Next.js is a web framework built on top of React and Node.js, allowing us to build web applications. Because it can run on the server, it can be used as a full-stack framework.

## Why Next.js?

Using Next.js has multiple benefits. We want to use it because of several reasons:

- **Very easy to get started with**: In the early days of React, it was very challenging to start a project. To get a simple page on the screen, we had to deal with many tools such as Webpack, Babel, and others. We still use those tools today, but fortunately, most tooling configuration is hidden from us with an interface to extend the configuration if required.

  Besides the challenges of setting up the project, it is very challenging to maintain all those dependencies over time. Next.js hides all those complexities away from developers and allows them to get started quickly with a new project.

- **Allows multiple rendering strategies**: Being able to use multiple rendering strategies is probably the main reason why we want to use Next.js, although it comes with other great benefits. First, it allows us to define the behavior of page rendering at the page level, meaning we can define how we want to render each page individually. It also supports multiple rendering strategies, such as the following:

  - Client-side rendering

  - Server-side rendering

  - Static site generation

  - Incremental static regeneration

  We will be using different strategies based on the application's needs.

- **Performance optimizations**: Next.js is built with web performance in mind. It implements performance optimization techniques such as the following:

  - Code splitting

  - Lazy loading

  - Prefetching

  - Image optimization

That sums up why we want to use Next.js for our application. Now, let's see what the Next.js application structure looks like.

## Next.js application structure

The easiest way to get started with Next.js is to use the `create-next-app` CLI to generate a new application.

Since we have already generated the application as part of the code samples, we do not need to use the CLI, but if we were generating the application from scratch, we would execute the following command:

```
npx create-next-app@latest jobs-app --typescript
```

By executing this command, we would generate a new Next.js application with TypeScript configured out of the box.

There are a couple of things that are specific to Next.js. Let's look at the following file and folder structure of a simple Next.js application:

```
- .next
- public
- src
  - pages
    - _app.tsx
    - index.tsx
- next.config.js
- package.json
```

Let's analyze each file and folder one by one:

- `.next`: Contains production-ready files generated by running the `build` command of Next.js.

- `public`: Contains all static assets of the application.

- `src/pages`: This is a special folder in Next.js where all pages defined here become available at corresponding routes. This is possible thanks to the filesystem-based routing system. The `pages` folder can also live in the root of the project, but it is nice to keep everything in the `src` folder.

- `src/pages/_app.tsx`: The `_app.tsx` file is a special file that exports a React component that wraps every page when rendered. By wrapping pages with this special component, we can add custom behavior for our application, such as adding any global configurations, providers, styles, layouts, and more to all the pages.

- `src/pages/index.tsx`: This is how we declare pages of the application. This shows how the root page is defined. We will dive into Next.js-specific routing in the upcoming chapters.

- `next.config.js`: This is where we can extend the default functionalities such as Webpack configuration and other things in a simple way.

- `package.json`: Every Next.js application includes the following npm scripts:

  - `dev`: Starts a development server on `localhost:3000`

  - `build`: Builds the application for production

  - `start`: Starts the production build on `localhost:3000`

We will cover more on these topics in the following chapters, but for now, this should give us enough information to get started with Next.js.

## TypeScript setup overview and usage

JavaScript is a dynamically typed programming language, meaning it doesn't catch any type errors during build time. That's where TypeScript comes into play.

TypeScript is a programming language that acts as a superset of JavaScript, which allows us to write JavaScript with some behaviors of a statically typed language. This comes in handy as we can catch many potential bugs before they get into production.

### Why TypeScript?

TypeScript is especially useful for large applications built by large teams. Code written in TypeScript is much better documented than code written in vanilla JavaScript. By looking at the type definitions, we can figure out how a piece of code is supposed to work.

Another reason is that TypeScript makes refactoring much easier because most of the issues can be caught before running the application.

TypeScript also helps us utilize our editor's IntelliSense, which shows us intelligent code completion, hover information, and signature information, which speeds up our productivity.

## TypeScript setup

Our project already has TypeScript configured. The TypeScript configuration is defined in the `tsconfig.json` file at the root of the project. It allows us to configure how strict we want it to be based on our needs:

```json
{
  "compilerOptions": {
    "target": "es5",
    "lib": ["dom", "dom.iterable", "esnext"],
    "allowJs": true,
    "skipLibCheck": true,
    "strict": true,
    "forceConsistentCasingInFileNames": true,
    "noEmit": true,
    "esModuleInterop": true,
    "module": "esnext",
    "moduleResolution": "Node",
    "resolveJsonModule": true,
    "isolatedModules": true,
    "jsx": "preserve",
    "incremental": true,
    "baseUrl": ".",
    "paths": {
      "@/*": ["./src/*"]
    }
  },
  "include": ["next-env.d.ts", "src"],
  "exclude": ["node_modules"]
}
```

We will not dive too deeply into every configuration property since most of the properties have been auto-generated. However, there is one thing that was also provided:

```json
  "baseUrl": ".",
  "paths": {
    "@/*": ["./src/*"]
  }
```

This will tell the TypeScript compiler that anything imported via @/* will refer to the src folder.

Previously, we had to perform messy imports, like so:

```
import { Component } from '../../../components/component'
```

Now, we can import components like so:

```
import { Component } from '@/components/component'
```

No matter how many nested levels we have, we can always import with absolute paths, and we will not be required to change our import statement should we decide to move the consumer file somewhere else.

## Basic TypeScript usage

Let's cover some TypeScript basics so that we are comfortable using it throughout this book.

### *Primitive types*

```
let numberVar: number;
numberVar = 1 // OK
numberVar = "1" // Error

let stringVar: string;
stringVar = "Hi"; // OK
stringVar = false; // Error

let stringVar: string;
stringVar = "Hi"; // OK
stringVar = false; // Error
```

As we can see, we are only allowed to assign values with the corresponding type. Assigning to any other type except the any type, which we will cover in a moment, will cause a TypeScript error.

### *Any*

The any type is the loosest type in TypeScript and using it will disable any type checking. We can use it when we want to bypass errors that would usually occur. However, we should only use it as a last resort and try to use other types first:

```
let anyVar: any;
anyVar = 1; // OK
anyVar = "Hello" // OK
```

```
anyVar = true; // OK
numberVar = anyVar; // OK
```

As we can see, variables with the any type can accept and be assigned to a value of any other type, which makes it very flexible.

### Unknown

Sometimes, we can't know upfront which types we will have. This might happen with some dynamic data where we don't know its type yet. Here, we can use the unknown type:

```
let unknownVar: unknown;
unknownVar = 1; // OK
unknownVar = "123" // OK

let unknownVar2: unknown;
unknownVar = unknownVar2; // OK
anyVar = unknownVar2; // OK
numberVar = unknownVar2; // Error
stringVar = unknownVar2; // Error
booleanVar = unknownVar2; // Error
```

As we can see, we can assign values of any type to the variable with unknown type. However, we can only assign values with type unknown to the variables with any and unknown types.

### Arrays

There are two ways to define array types with TypeScript:

```
type numbers = number[]
type strings = Array<string>
```

### Objects

Object shapes can be defined in two ways:

```
type Person = {
  name: string;
  age: number;
}

interface Person {
```

```
  name: string;
  age: number;
}
```

The first one is called type alias, while the second is called interface.

There are a few differences between type aliases and interfaces, but we won't get into them right now. For any object shape type we define, we can use type aliases.

## Unions

The basic types we just mentioned are great, but sometimes, we want to allow a variable to be one of many types. Let's look at the following example:

```
type Content = string | number;
let content: Content;
content = 1 // OK
content = "Hi"; // OK
content = false // Error
```

As we can see, the `content` variable can now be either `string` or `number`.

We can also add literal types in the union, as shown in the following example:

```
type Color = "red" | "green" | "blue";
let color: Color;
color = "red" // OK
color = "yellow" // Error
```

Here, we are defining colors as strings, but we want to add more constraints so that we can only take one of those three colors. If we try to add anything else, TypeScript will warn us with an error.

## Intersections

Intersection types allow us to combine the properties of two different objects into a single type. Consider this example:

```
type Foo = {
  x: string;
  y: number;
}

type Bar = {
```

```
    z: boolean;
}


type FooBar = Foo & Bar;
```

The FooBar type will now contain the x, y, and z properties.

## Generics

Generics is a mechanism of creating reusable types by parameterizing them. They can help us reduce code repetition. Consider the following type:

```
type Foo = {
    x: number;
}
```

Let's see what happens if we need the same structure but with x as a string:

```
type Foo = {
    x: string;
}
```

Here, we can see that there is some code duplication going on. We can simplify this by making it generic so that it accepts the type as T. This would be assigned as the type of the x property:

```
type Foo<T> = {
    x: T;
}


let x: Foo<number>;
let y: Foo<string>;
```

Now, we have a nice way to reuse the structure by passing different types to the generic.

We can also use generics with functions:

```
function logger<T>(value: T) {
    console.log(value)
}


logger<number>(1) // OK
logger<string>(1); // Error
```

To try out these snippets and see how different types behave, go to `https://www.typescriptlang.org/play`, copy the snippets, and play around with the types to see how they work.

### TypeScript and React

Every TypeScript file that uses JSX must have the `.tsx` extension.

Typing React components is very straightforward:

```
type InfoProps = {
  name: string;
  age: number
};


const Info = (props: InfoProps) => {
  return <div>{props.name}-{props.age}</div>;
};
```

These examples are pretty trivial. We will see more practical examples in the upcoming chapters when we start building the application. To learn more about TypeScript, it is recommended to check the TypeScript handbook at `https://www.typescriptlang.org/docs`, which covers all these topics in much more detail.

## ESLint setup overview

**Linting** is a process where linters analyze source code and detect any potential issues in the code base.

We will be using **ESLint**, which is the most popular linting tool for JavaScript. It can be configured with different plugins and rules to adapt the linter to our application's needs.

The ESLint configuration is defined in the `.eslintrc.js` file at the root of the project. We can add different rules, extend them with different plugins, and override which files to apply the rules to so that they suit our application's needs.

Sometimes, we don't want to lint every folder and file, so we can tell ESLint to ignore folders and files by defining them in the `.eslintignore` file.

ESLint has great integration with editors and IDEs so that we can see any potential issues in the file while we are coding.

To run our linter, we have defined the linting script in `package.json`:

```
"lint": "eslint --ext .ts,.tsx ./src",
```

By running npm run lint, we will lint every .ts and .tsx file in the src directory, and the linter will notify us about any potential issues.

## Prettier setup overview

**Prettier** is a great tool for formatting code. It enforces a consistent coding style across the entire code base. By utilizing the "format on save" feature in our IDE, we can automatically format the code based on the configuration provided in the .prettierrc file. It will also give us good feedback when something is wrong with the code. If it doesn't auto-format, something is wrong with the code and it needs to be fixed.

Prettier comes with a default configuration out of the box. We can override this by creating the .prettierrc file and modifying the configuration.

Just as with ESLint, sometimes, there are files we do not want to auto-format. We can tell Prettier to ignore files and folders by adding them to the .prettierignore file.

To run Prettier, we have defined a couple of scripts in package.json:

```
"prettier": "prettier \"**/*.+(json|ts|tsx)\"",
"format:check": "npm run prettier -- --check",
"format:fix": "npm run prettier -- --write",
```

As we can see, we can run npm run format:check to just check the formatting without trying to fix it. If we want to fix it, then we can run npm run format:fix, which will modify the files that need to be fixed.

## Pre-committing checks setup overview

Having static code analysis tools such as TypeScript, ESLint, and Prettier is great; we have configured them and can run individual scripts whenever we make some changes to ensure everything is in the best order.

However, there are some drawbacks. Developers can forget to run all checks before committing to the repo, which can still bring problematic and inconsistent code to production.

Fortunately, there is a solution that can fix this problem: whenever we try to commit to the repository, we want to run all checks in an automated way.

This is the flow we want to have:

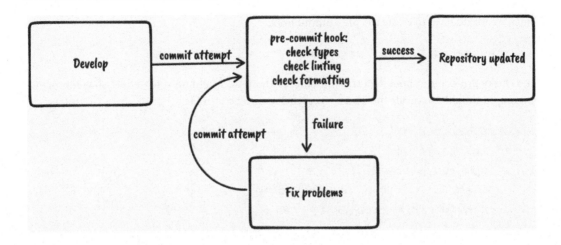

Figure 2.1 – Pre-commit code checking diagram

As we can see, whenever we attempt to commit to the repository, the `git pre-commit` hook will run and execute the scripts that will do the checking. If all the checks pass, the changes will be committed to the repository; otherwise, we will have to fix the issues and try again.

To enable this flow, we will use `husky` and `lint-staged`:

- `husky` is a tool that allows us to run git hooks. We want to run the pre-commit hook to run the checks before committing our changes.

- `lint-staged` is a tool that allows us to run those checks only on files that are in the staging area of Git. This improves the speed of code checking since doing that on the entire code base might be too slow.

We already have these tools installed and configured, but if we didn't, they could be installed using the following command:

```
npm install --save-dev husky lint-staged
```

Then, we would need to enable Git hooks:

```
npx husky install
```

Then, we would need to create the pre-commit hook:

```
npx husky add .husky/pre-commit "npx lint-staged"
```

The Husky pre-commit hook will run lint-staged. Then, we would need to define what commands lint-staged should run inside the `lint-staged.config.js` file:

```
module.exports = {
  '*.{ts,tsx}': [
    'npm run lint',
    "bash -c 'npm run types:check'",
    'npm run format:check',
  ],
};
```

If we try to commit code that contains any violations, it will fail and stop us from committing the changes.

Now that we covered most of our setup, let's look at the structure of our project.

# Project structure overview

As we already mentioned, React is very flexible when it comes to project structure.

Some of the benefits of having a good project structure are as follows:

- Separation of concerns
- Easier refactors
- Better reasoning about the code base
- Easier for larger teams to work on the code base simultaneously

Let's see what the feature-based project structure looks like.

> **Note**
> We will focus on the `src` folder only since, from now on, most of the code base lives there.

Here is the structure of our `src` folder:

```
- components // (1)
- config // (2)
- features // (3)
- layouts // (4)
- lib // (5)
- pages // (6)
- providers // (7)
- stores // (8)
- testing // (9)
- types // (10)
- utils // (11)
```

Let's analyze each of the folders, one by one:

1.  `components`: Contains all shared components that are used across the entire application.

2.  `config`: Contains the application configuration files.

3.  `features`: Contains all the feature-based modules. We will analyze this one in more detail in the following section.

4.  `layouts`: Contains different layouts for the pages.

5.  `lib`: Contains configurations for different libraries that are used in our application.

6.  `pages`: Contains the pages of our application. This is where Next.js will look for pages in the filesystem-based routing.

7.  `providers`: Contains all application providers. For example, if our application uses many different providers for styling, state, and so on, we can combine them here and export a single application provider with which we can wrap our `_app.tsx` to make all the providers available on all the pages.

8.  `stores`: Contains all global state stores that are used in the application.

9.  `testing`: Contains test-related mocks, helpers, utilities, and configurations.

10. `types`: Contains base TypeScript type definitions that are used across the application.

11. `utils`: Contains all shared utility functions.

There is nothing wrong with grouping files in folders based on their types. However, once the application starts to grow, it becomes more difficult to reason about and maintain the code base because there are too many files of a single type.

## Features

To scale the application in the easiest and most maintainable way, we want to keep most of the application code inside the `features` folder, which should contain different feature-based things. Every `feature` folder should contain domain-specific code for a given feature. This will allow us to keep functionalities scoped to a feature and not mix its declarations with the shared things. This is much easier to maintain than a flat folder structure with many files.

Let's look at one of our feature folders, which has the following structure:

```
- api // (1)
- components // (2)
- types // (3)
- index.ts // (4)
```

1.  `api`: Contains the API request declarations and API hooks related to a specific feature. This makes our API layer and the UI layer separate and reusable.

2.  `components`: Contains all components that are scoped to a specific feature.

3.  `types`: This contains the TypeScript type definitions for a specific feature.

4.  `index.ts`: This is the entry point of every feature. It behaves as the public API of the feature, and it should only export things that should be public for other parts of the application.

> **Note**
>
> A feature might have other folders, such as `hooks`, `utils`, and others, depending on the needs of the feature. The only required file is the `index.ts` file, which acts as the public API of a feature.

Let's try to visualize the project structure with the following diagram:

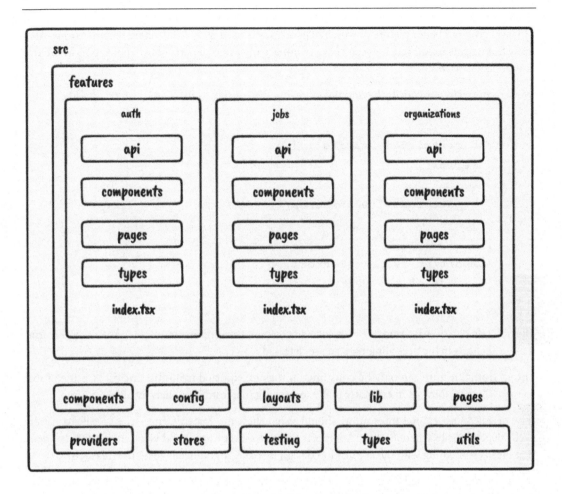

Figure 2.2 – Project structure

As we can see, most of our application code will live within features.

One more thing we can configure is enforcing developers to import features code via the index.
ts file, like so:

```
import {JobsList} from '@/features/jobs'
```

We shouldn't do this:

```
import {JobsList} from '@/features/jobs/components/jobs-
  list'
```

This will give us a better picture of which dependency is used where and where it comes from. Also, if the feature gets refactored, it doesn't have to impact any external parts of the application where that component is used.

We can constrain our code by having the following ESLint rule in the `.eslintrc.js` file:

```
rules: {
    'no-restricted-imports': [
      'error',
      {
        patterns: ['@/features/*/*'],
      },
    ],
    'import/no-cycle': 'error',
    … rest of the eslint rules
}
```

The `no-restricted-imports` rule will add constraints to imports from other features by erroring if any violations in the preceding pattern are detected.

Things from a feature can only be consumed if they're exported from the `index.ts` file of that feature. This will force us to explicitly make something in a feature publicly available.

If we decide to use features this way, we should also include the `import/no-cycle` rule to prevent cyclic dependencies where Feature A imports things from Feature B and vice versa. If this happens, that means something with the application design is wrong and it needs to be restructured.

In this section, we learned what our application structure will look like. Then, we focused on splitting the application by feature, which will allow our code base to scale well if we decide to add more features.

## Summary

In this chapter, we learned the basics of our Next.js application setup, which has been configured to work with TypeScript. Then, we learned about absolute imports, which will make it easier to move files around. We also overviewed ESLint and Prettier and made them static code analysis tools so that they can run checks before committing the changes to our repository by using lint-staged and Husky.

Finally, we learned what our project structure will look like. We learned that the best way is to group code by features. We also defined an ESLint rule to enforce importing code from a feature in a specific way and prevent cyclic dependencies to make the code base clean and easy to reason about.

In the next chapter, we will create the shared components that will act as the baseline for our application's user interface.

# 3
# Building and Documenting Components

In React, everything is a component. This paradigm allows us to split user interfaces into smaller parts, thus making it easier to develop applications. It also enables component reusability since we can reuse the same components in multiple places.

In this chapter, we will build some components that we will use as the application's user interface base. This will make the application UI more consistent and easier to understand and maintain. We will also learn how to document the components with Storybook, a great tool that can serve as a catalog of common application components.

In this chapter, we will cover the following topics:

- Chakra UI
- Building components
- Storybook
- Documenting components

By the end of this chapter, we will learn how to create and document reusable components that we can use for the application.

# Technical requirements

Before we get started, we need to set up the project. To be able to develop the project, you will need the following things installed on your computer:

- **Node.js** version 16 or above and **npm** version 8 or above.

  There are multiple ways to install Node.js and npm. Here is a great article that goes into more detail: `https://www.nodejsdesignpatterns.com/blog/5-ways-to-install-node-js`

- **VSCode** (optional) is currently the most popular editor/IDE for JavaScript/TypeScript, so we will be using it. It is open source, has great integration with TypeScript, and you can extend its features via extensions. It can be downloaded from here: `https://code.visualstudio.com/`.

The code files for this chapter can be found here: `https://github.com/PacktPublishing/React-Application-Architecture-for-Production`.

The repository can be cloned locally with the following command:

```
git clone https://github.com/PacktPublishing/React-Application-
Architecture-for-Production.git
```

Once the repository is cloned, we need to install the application's dependencies:

```
npm install
```

We also need to provide the environment variables:

```
cp .env.example .env
```

Once the dependencies have been installed, we need to select the right stage of the code base that matches this chapter. We can do that by executing the following command:

```
npm run stage:switch
```

This command will prompt us with a list of stages for each chapter:

```
? What stage do you want to switch to? (Use arrow
  keys)
> chapter-02
  chapter-03
  chapter-03-start
  chapter-04
```

```
  chapter-04-start
  chapter-05
  chapter-05-start
(Move up and down to reveal more choices)
```

This is the third chapter, so you can select `chapter-03-start` if you want to follow along or `chapter-03` to see the final results of the chapter.

Once the chapter has been selected, all files required to follow along with the chapter will appear.

To follow along with this chapter, you don't need to make any changes to the code. You can use it as a reference to help get a better overview of the code base.

For more information about the setup details, check out the `README.md` file.

# Chakra UI

Whenever we build a UI for an application, we must decide what to use for styling our components. In addition, we must also consider whether we want to make all components from scratch or use a component library with pre-made components.

The advantage of using a component library is that it gives us a productivity boost as we don't have to implement components that have already been implemented, such as buttons, dialogs, and tabs. Also, some libraries come with great accessibility defaults out of the box, so we don't have to think about it as much as we would if we built everything from scratch. These libraries can come with costs, such as difficult customizability or a significant impact on the final bundle size. On the other hand, they save us a lot of development time.

For our application, we will use **Chakra UI**, a component library built on top of a combination of **emotion** and **styled-system**, which will allow us to write CSS in JavaScript in a consistent way.

## Chakra UI setup

We already have the Chakra UI library installed, and now we need to configure it.

To use Chakra UI, first, we need to configure its theme provider to enable styles for its components. Since all our providers and wrappers are defined in `src/providers/app.tsx`, we can add `ChakraProvider` there:

```
import {
  ChakraProvider,
  GlobalStyle,
} from '@chakra-ui/react';
```

```
import { ReactNode } from 'react';

import { theme } from '@/config/theme';

type AppProviderProps = {
  children: ReactNode;
};

export const AppProvider = ({
  children,
}: AppProviderProps) => {
  return (
    <ChakraProvider theme={theme}>
      <GlobalStyle />
      {children}
    </ChakraProvider>
  );
};
```

Here, we are wrapping the entire application with the provider to apply theming and styles to all Chakra UI components. We are also rendering the GlobalStyles component, which will take any global styles from our theme and apply it to the application.

Chakra UI settings and components are very customizable and can be configured in a custom theme, which we can pass to the provider. It will override the default theme configuration. Let's configure the theme in src/config/theme.ts by adding the following:

```
import { extendTheme } from '@chakra-ui/react';

const colors = {
  primary: '#1a365d',
  primaryAccent: '#ffffff',
};

const styles = {
  global: {
    'html, body': {
      height: '100%',
```

```
      bg: 'gray.50',
    },

    '#__next': {
      height: '100%',
      bg: 'gray.50',
    },
  },
};
export const theme = extendTheme({ colors, styles });
```

We are defining some global styles that will be injected via the `GlobalStyles` component, which we have already added in `AppProvider`. We also define the theme colors we want to have available in the components. Then, we combine these configurations with the default theme values by using the `extendTheme` utility, which will merge all configurations and give us the complete theme object.

It is useful to centralize theme configuration since it is easy to use and change if the branding of the application changes. For example, we can easily change the primary color value in one place and apply it to the entire application without any additional changes.

## Building components

Now that the Chakra UI setup is in place, we can build the components. In the starting files for this chapter, we already have some default components exported. For now, we can render them on the landing page defined in `src/pages/index.tsx` as follows:

```
import { Button } from '@/components/button';
import { InputField } from '@/components/form';
import { Link } from '@/components/link';

const LandingPage = () => {
  return (
    <>
      <Button />
      <br />
      <InputField />
      <br />
      <Link />
    </>
```

```
  );
};
```

```
export default LandingPage;
```

To start the application development server, we need to run the following:

```
npm run dev
```

This will make the newly created page available at http://localhost:3000. The development server will listen to any changes we make and auto-refresh the page with the latest changes.

The landing page will display the components. If we open http://localhost:3000, we should see the following:

Figure 3.1 – Preview of the initial components on the landing page

The components aren't doing much right now, so we need to work on their implementation.

## Button

Let's start by implementing the Button component, one of the most common components in every application. The component is already created in src/components/button/button.tsx, but we need to modify it.

Let's start by importing its dependencies:

```
import { Button as ChakraButton } from '@chakra-ui/react';
import { MouseEventHandler, ReactNode } from 'react';
```

Now, we can create the `variants` object, which will hold all styling properties of our button and they will be applied accordingly to the default Chakra UI `Button` component:

```
const variants = {
  solid: {
    variant: 'solid',
    bg: 'primary',
    color: 'primaryAccent',
    _hover: {
      opacity: '0.9',
    },
  },
  outline: {
    variant: 'outline',
    bg: 'white',
    color: 'primary',
  },
};
```

Then, we can type the props for the `Button` component:

```
export type ButtonProps = {
  children: ReactNode;
  type?: 'button' | 'submit' | 'reset';
  variant?: keyof typeof variants;
  isLoading?: boolean;
  isDisabled?: boolean;
  onClick?: MouseEventHandler<HTMLButtonElement>;
  icon?: JSX.Element;
};
```

Typing the component's props is a great way to describe its API, which is very useful as it documents how it should be used.

And now, we can create the `Button` component, which is just a wrapper around the default `Button` component provided by Chakra UI:

```
export const Button = ({
  variant = 'solid',
  type = 'button',
  children,
  icon,
  ...props
}: ButtonProps) => {
  return (
    <ChakraButton
      {...props}
      {...variants[variant]}
      type={type}
      leftIcon={icon}
    >
      {children}
    </ChakraButton>
  );
};
```

Then, we can update the `Button` component usage in `src/pages/index.tsx` as follows:

```
<Button variant="solid" type="button">
  Click Me
</Button>
```

## InputField

The input field component is an input component that we want to use when building our forms. Let's change `src/components/form/input-field.tsx`.

First, we need to import all dependencies:

```
import {
  FormControl,
  FormHelperText,
  FormLabel,
```

```
  forwardRef,
  Input,
  Textarea,
} from '@chakra-ui/react';
import {
  FieldError,
  UseFormRegister,
} from 'react-hook-form';
```

Then, we define types for the component's props:

```
export type InputFieldProps = {
  type?: 'text' | 'email' | 'password' | 'textarea';
  label?: string;
  error?: FieldError;
} & Partial<
  ReturnType<UseFormRegister<Record<string, unknown>>>
>;
```

Finally, we implement the component itself:

```
export const InputField = forwardRef(
  (props: InputFieldProps, ref) => {
    const {
      type = 'text',
      label,
      error,
      ...inputProps
    } = props;

    return (
      <FormControl>
        {label && <FormLabel>{label}</FormLabel>}
        {type === 'textarea' ? (
          <Textarea
            bg="white"
            rows={8}
            {...inputProps}
```

```
                    ref={ref}
                />
            ) : (
                <Input
                    bg="white"
                    type={type}
                    {...inputProps}
                    ref={ref}
                />
            )}
            {error && (
                <FormHelperText color="red">
                    {error.message}
                </FormHelperText>
            )}
        </FormControl>
    );
    }
);
```

As you can see, we are building an input field component that we can use with the react-hook-form library to create forms, and we will learn how to do that in the upcoming chapters. Notice how we are wrapping the component with forwardRef. This will allow us to pass references to the component if necessary.

Let's update its usage in src/pages/index.tsx:

```
<InputField label="Name" />
```

## Link

For the links, we will use the Link component provided by Next.js. However, we want to centralize the configuration and styling and use it everywhere. Let's modify src/components/link/link.tsx:

First, let's import all dependencies:

```
import { Button } from '@chakra-ui/react';
import NextLink from 'next/link';
import { ReactNode } from 'react';
```

Similar to what we did with the `Button` component, we want to allow the link to accept some variants, which will apply additional styling props to the component:

```
const variants = {
  link: {
    variant: 'link',
    color: 'primary',
  },
  solid: {
    variant: 'solid',
    bg: 'primary',
    color: 'primaryAccent',
    _hover: {
      opacity: '0.9',
    },
  },
  outline: {
    variant: 'outline',
    color: 'primary',
    bg: 'white',
  },
};
```

Then, we define the type of the component's props:

```
export type LinkProps = {
  href: string;
  children: ReactNode;
  variant?: keyof typeof variants;
  icon?: JSX.Element;
  shallow?: boolean;
};
```

And here is the implementation of the `Link` component. Notice how we are using the `Link` component from Next.js, which we use to wrap the `Button` component from Chakra UI:

```
export const Link = (({
  href,
  children,
```

```
    variant = 'link',
    icon,
    shallow = false,
  }: LinkProps) => {
    return (
      <NextLink shallow={shallow} href={href} passHref>
        <Button
          leftIcon={icon}
          as="a"
          {...variants[variant]}
        >
          {children}
        </Button>
      </NextLink>
    );
  };
```

Why are we using the `Button` component instead of `Link` from Chakra UI? We could have used `Link`, but we want most of our links to look and feel like buttons, so the reason is just the style preference. Notice how we are passing `as="a"` to `Button`. This will make the element an anchor, which is correct from the accessibility standpoint, and the component will be rendered as a link element in the DOM.

Let's update its usage in `src/pages/index.tsx`:

```
<Link href="/">Home</Link>
```

Note that we can't predict and build all shared components upfront. Sometimes we realize that something needs to be abstracted while we are developing it. It is also challenging to anticipate all edge cases of a component, so abstracting it too early might complicate things in the long run.

For now, we have abstracted the most generic components we will surely use as they are.

Remember, the implementation details of each component don't matter. If you don't understand everything they are doing and how they work, it's okay. The key takeaway is that we want to abstract the most common components so we can reuse them when needed.

Since most component libraries are very generic, with many options to fit everyone's needs, it is a good idea to make our wrappers around their default components to reduce the default API surface and adapt them to the application's needs. This will reduce the overhead of components with too many configuration options and props we will never use. Also, it will bring consistency since developers are constrained to using fewer options.

Let's look at our index page where the components are rendered:

Figure 3.2 – Preview of the components on the landing page

Great! Now go ahead and try to play around with different props and see how the components behave.

Our components are working correctly and are ready to be used in the application. However, there are a couple of issues:

- We are occupying the index route. What happens when we want to use it for something meaningful, such as the landing page? We will not be able to use that page for previewing our components. Sure, we can create and use another page that will never be used, but that is not a very good option either.

- We don't want to display all components together as it is messy, and it would be better to try them out in isolation.

- We want to play around with the component props, which is impossible with the current approach since we would have to modify the code.

Let's see in the next section how we can solve these issues and develop and try components in isolation without changing our application's code.

# Storybook

**Storybook** is a tool that allows us to develop and test UI components in isolation. We can think of it as a tool for making catalogs of all the components we have. It is great for documenting components. A couple of benefits of using Storybook include the following:

- Storybook allows developing components in isolation without the need to reproduce the exact state of the application, allowing developers to focus on the things they are building

- Storybook serves as a catalog of UI components allowing all stakeholders to try out the components without using them in the application

Storybook is configured by using the following command:

```
npx storybook init
```

This command will install all required dependencies and set up the configuration that resides in the .storybook folder at the root of the project.

## Storybook configuration

We already have Storybook installed, so let's look at the configuration, which has two files.

The first file contains the main configuration, which controls how the Storybook server behaves and how it processes our stories. It lives in .storybook/main.js:

```
const path = require('path');
const TsconfigPathsPlugin = require('tsconfig-paths-webpack-
plugin');

module.exports = {
  stories: ['../src/**/*.stories.tsx'],
  addons: [
    '@storybook/addon-links',
    '@storybook/addon-essentials',
    '@storybook/addon-interactions',
    '@chakra-ui/storybook-addon',
  ],
  features: {
    emotionAlias: false,
  },
  framework: '@storybook/react',
```

```
  core: {
    builder: '@storybook/builder-webpack5',
  },
  webpackFinal: async (config) => {
    config.resolve.plugins = config.resolve.plugins || [];
    config.resolve.plugins.push(
      new TsconfigPathsPlugin({
        configFile: path.resolve(
          __dirname,
          '../tsconfig.json'
        ),
      })
    );
    return config;
  },
};
```

The main configuration contains the following properties:

- `stories`: An array of globs that indicates the locations of our stories.

- `addons`: A list of add-ons used to enhance the default behavior of Storybook.

- `features`: Enables Storybook's additional features.

- `framework`: Framework-specific configurations.

- `core`: Internal feature configuration.

- `webpackFinal`: Configuration for extending default webpack configuration. We are enabling absolute imports by telling Storybook to use paths from the `tsconfig.json` file.

The second configuration file controls how the stories are rendered in the UI. This configuration lives in `.storybook/preview.js`:

```
import { theme } from '../src/config/theme';
export const parameters = {
  actions: { argTypesRegex: '^on[A-Z].*' },
  controls: {
    matchers: {
      color: /(background|color)$/i,
      date: /Date$/,
```

```
    },
  },
  controls: { expanded: true },
  chakra: {
    theme,
  },
};
```

Notice how we are passing the theme to the `chakra` property in `parameters`. This will enable Chakra theming to be applied to our components in Storybook.

We can optionally export decorators, which will wrap all the stories. It is useful if the components rely on some providers that we want to have available in all stories.

## Storybook scripts

Our Storybook setup has two npm scripts:

- Running Storybook in development

  To start the development server, we can execute the following command:

  **`npm run storybook`**

  The command will open Storybook at `http://localhost:6006/`.

- Building Storybook for production

  We can also generate and deploy the stories to be visible without running the development server. To build the stories, we can execute the following command:

  **`npm run storybook:build`**

  Generated files can then be found in the `storybook-static` folder, and they can be deployed anywhere.

Now that we have familiarized ourselves with the setup, it's time to write the stories for the components.

## Documenting components

If we recall from the previous section, the configuration in `.storybook/main.js` has the `stories` property as follows:

```
stories: ['../src/**/*.stories.tsx']
```

This means that any file in the `src` folder that ends with `.stories.tsx` should be picked by Storybook and treated as a story. With that said, we will co-locate stories next to the components, so the structure for every component will look something like this:

```
components
  my-component
    my-component.stories.tsx
    my-component.tsx
    index.ts
```

We will create our stories based on **Component Story Format** (**CSF**), an open standard for writing component examples.

But first, what is a story? According to the CSF standard, a story should represent a single source of truth for a component. We can think of a story as a user story where a component is presented in the corresponding state.

CSF requires the following:

- Default exports should define metadata about a component, including the component itself, the component's name, decorators, and parameters
- Named exports should define all stories

Let's now create the stories for the components.

## Button stories

To create stories for the `Button` component, we need to create an `src/components/button/button.stories.tsx` file.

Then, we can start by adding the required imports:

```
import { PlusSquareIcon } from '@chakra-ui/icons';
import { Meta, Story } from '@storybook/react';


import { Button, ButtonProps } from './button';
```

Then, we create the meta configuration object:

```
const meta: Meta = {
  title: 'Components/Button',
  component: Button,
```

```
};

export default meta;
```

Notice that we are exporting it as a default export. This is what Storybook requires, according to CSF.

Since we can have multiple stories, we must create a story template:

```
const Template: Story<ButtonProps> = (props) => (
  <Button {...props} />
);
```

And then we can export the first story:

```
export const Default = Template.bind({});

Default.args = {
  children: 'Click Me',
};
```

We can pass any props we need to the `args` object attached to the story, which will be reflected in our stories in Storybook.

We can do the same thing for another story where we want to have a version of `Button` that has an icon:

```
export const WithIcon = Template.bind({});
WithIcon.args = {
  children: 'Click Me',
  icon: <PlusSquareIcon />,
};
```

To see the story, let's execute the following command:

**npm run storybook**

Now, let's visit http://localhost:6006/:

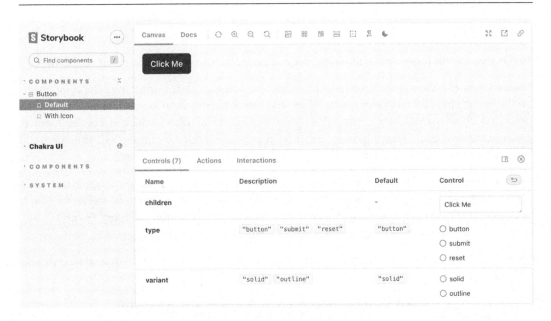

Figure 3.3 – Button component story

And there, we have the Button component previewed in isolation. Notice the control panel at the bottom. This gives us a friendly interface to play with the component's props without touching the code.

Isn't this much nicer than what we had first with rendering components on the index page? We can deploy stories anywhere and allow non-technical people to experiment with the components without coding knowledge.

## Exercises

To solidify your understanding of Storybook, let's have a go at some exercises. Go ahead and create stories for the following components:

- InputField:
  - Default story
  - With error story
- Link:
  - Default story
  - With icon story

# Summary

In this chapter, our focus was on building base components that we will reuse in our application.

We started by configuring the Chakra UI provider and theming. Then we displayed the components on the landing page for testing purposes. They were not doing much, so we implemented them. The point of defining shared components is that we can reuse them anywhere, which makes development easier in the long run. What the components are doing here is not very important. The important thing is to think about creating shared components as a base for the application.

We then needed to preview the components somewhere and since doing that on a page is not a very elegant solution, we chose Storybook. We covered its configuration, and then we defined a couple of stories for the Button component. The stories are written in **Component Story Format (CSF)**, which is a standard for how to write component examples.

As an exercise at the end of this chapter, there were further stories to implement, which should solidify all learnings so far.

In the next chapter, we will use these components when we start creating our pages.

# 4

# **Building and Configuring Pages**

In the previous chapters, we have configured the base of our application, including the setup of the application, and shared UI components that will serve as the foundation of our UI.

In this chapter, we can proceed by creating our application pages. We will learn how routing in Next.js works and what rendering methods we can use to get the most out of Next.js. Then, we will learn about configuring per-page layouts, making our application look and feel like a single-page application.

In this chapter, we will cover the following topics:

- Next.js routing
- Next.js rendering strategies
- Next.js SEO
- Layouts
- Building the pages

By the end of this chapter, we will learn how to create pages in Next.js and get a better understanding of selecting different rendering strategies depending on the needs of the application.

## Technical requirements

Before we get started, we need to set up the project. To be able to develop the project, you will need the following things installed on your computer:

- **Node.js** version 16 or above and **npm** version 8 or above.

  There are multiple ways to install Node.js and npm. Here is a great article that goes into more detail:

  `https://www.nodejsdesignpatterns.com/blog/5-ways-to-install-node-js`

- **VSCode** (optional) is currently the most popular editor/IDE for JavaScript/TypeScript, so we will be using it. It is open source, has great integration with TypeScript, and you can extend its features via extensions. It can be downloaded from `https://code.visualstudio.com/`.

The code files for this chapter can be found here: `https://github.com/PacktPublishing/ React-Application-Architecture-for-Production`

The repository can be cloned locally with the following command:

```
git clone https://github.com/PacktPublishing/React-Application-
Architecture-for-Production.git
```

Once the repository is cloned, we need to install the application's dependencies:

```
npm install
```

We also need to provide the environment variables:

```
cp .env.example .env
```

Once the dependencies have been installed, we need to select the right stage of the code base that matches this chapter. We can do that by executing the following command:

```
npm run stage:switch
```

This command will prompt us with a list of stages for each chapter:

```
? What stage do you want to switch to? (Use arrow
  keys)
> chapter-02
  chapter-03
  chapter-03-start
  chapter-04
  chapter-04-start
  chapter-05
  chapter-05-start
(Move up and down to reveal more choices)
```

This is the fourth chapter, so you can select `chapter-04-start` if you want to follow along, or `chapter-04` to see the final results of the chapter. Once the chapter has been selected, all files required to follow along with the chapter will appear.

To follow along with this chapter, you don't need to make any changes to the code. You can use it as a reference to help get a better overview of the code base.

For more information about the setup details, check out the README.md file.

## Next.js routing

Next.js has a filesystem-based router where every page file represents a page. The pages are special files that exist in the pages folder, and they have the following structure:

```
const Page = () => {
    return <div>Welcome to the page!</div>
}
export default Page;
```

As you can see, only exporting the page component as a default export is required; this is the minimum requirement for a page to be defined. We will see what else can be exported from a page in a few moments.

Since the routing is filesystem-based, routes are determined by how the page files are named. For example, the page pointing to the root route should be defined in the src/pages/index.tsx file. If we want the about page, we can define it in src/pages/about.tsx.

For any complex application with dynamic data, it is not enough to only create predefined pages. For example, let's say we have a social network application where we can visit user profiles. The profiles should be loaded by the user's ID. Since it would be too repetitive to create a page file for every user, we need to make the page dynamic as follows:

```
// pages/users/[userId].tsx
import { useRouter } from 'next/router';

const UserProfile = () => {
    const router = useRouter();
    const userId = router.query.userId;
    return <div>User: {userId}</div>;
}


export default UserProfile
```

To get the ID and load the data dynamically, we can define a generic user profile page in pages/users/[userId].tsx, where userId will be injected into the page dynamically. For example, going to /users/123 will show the user profile page and pass the value of 123 as userId via the query property of the router.

# Next.js rendering strategies

Next.js supports four different rendering strategies:

- **Client-side rendering**: Where we can load the initial content on the server and then fetch additional data from the client.

- **Server-side rendering**: Where we can fetch the data on the server, inject it on the page, and return the page to the client with the provided data.

- **Static site generation**: Where static data is injected on the page and returned in the markup to the client.

- **Incremental static regeneration**: The middle ground between server-side rendering and static site generation. We can generate $x$ number of pages statically, and then if a page that hasn't been rendered and cached yet is requested, Next.js can render it on the server and cache it for future requests.

For our application, we will mainly focus on the first two methods, so let's see how they work in the following examples.

## Client-side rendering

Considering the user profile page example, we can perform client-side rendering by writing the pages as follows:

```
// pages/users/[userId].tsx
import { useRouter } from 'next/router';
import { useUser } from './api';

const UserProfile = () => {
    const router = useRouter();
    const userId = router.query.userId;
    const { user, isLoading } = useUser(userId);

    if(!user && isLoading) return <div>Loading...</div>;

    if(!user) return <div>User not found!</div>;

    return <div>User: {user.name}</div>;
}
```

As we can see, we are using `userId` to fetch the user data. In this example, we are doing this on the client side, which means that the server will initially render the following markup:

```
<div>Loading...</div>
```

Only after the data is fetched on the client will the user data be displayed:

```
<div>User: {user.name}</div>
```

This is fine unless we care about SEO and the performance of the initial page load. Here we have to wait for the initial page to load and then for the user data to be fetched. This approach is perfectly valid for data that is not supposed to be public, such as admin dashboards.

However, for public pages, it is a good idea to enable the server to return the actual markup to the client to make it easier for search engines to crawl and index our pages. We can do that by server-side rendering the pages.

## Server-side rendering

Let's revisit the user profile page example, this time by rendering it on the server:

```
// pages/users/[userId].tsx
import { useRouter } from 'next/router';
import { getUser } from './api';

const UserProfile = ({ user }) => {
    const router = userRouter();
    const userId = router.query;
    const { user } = useUser(userId);

    if(!user) return <div>User not found!</div>;

    return <div>User: {user.name}</div>;
}

export const getServerSideProps = async ({ params }) => {
    const userId = params.userId;
    const user = await getUser(userId);

    return {
```

```
        props: {
              user
        }
    }
}
```

As we can see here, besides the page component, the page file exports the getServerSideProps function, which is executed on the server. Its return value can contain props, which is passed to the component's props.

The server will render the following markup:

```
<div>User: {user.name}</div>
```

The complete markup with the user data will be available on the initial render.

Let's keep in mind that there is no perfect rendering strategy for all use cases; therefore, we must balance the pros and cons and choose which one to use based on our needs. The great thing with Next.js is that it allows us to use different rendering strategies per page so we can combine them to fit the application's needs in the best way.

## Next.js SEO

To improve the SEO of our pages, we should add some meta tags and the title of the page and inject them into the page. This can be done via the Head component provided by Next.js.

For the application, we want to have a dedicated component where we can add the title of the pages. Let's open the src/components/seo/seo.tsx file and add the following:

```
import Head from 'next/head';

export type SeoProps = {
  title: string;
};

export const Seo = ({ title }: SeoProps) => {
  return (
    <Head>
      <title>{title}</title>
    </Head>
  );
};
```

The Head component will inject its content into the head of the page. For now, the title will suffice, but it can be extended to add different meta tags if needed.

Let's add the Seo component to our landing page at `src/pages/index.tsx`.

First, let's import the component:

```
import { Seo } from '@/components/seo';
```

And then, we can add it at the top of the component:

```
const LandingPage = () => {
  return (
    <>
      <Seo title="Jobs App" />
      <Center>
      {/* rest of the component */}
      </Center>
    </>
  );
};
export default LandingPage
```

## Layouts

When developing an application with multiple views or pages, we need to consider layout reusability.

Consider the following example:

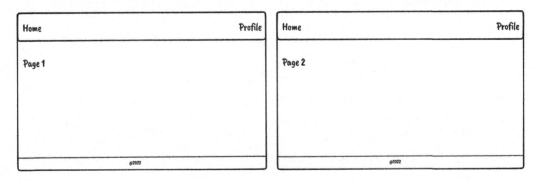

Figure 4.1 – Layouts example

We can see that the navbar and the footer are the same on both pages and the main content comes between, so it is a good idea to make it reusable.

There are two ways to add the layout component to pages:

- Wrap the returned JSX of every page with the layout component
- Attach the layout to the page component and use it to wrap the entire component

## Wrapping JSX of every page with the layout component

Let's say we have a layout component that can wrap the content of each page:

```
const Layout = ({ children }) => {
    return (
        <div>
            <Header />
            {children}
            <Footer />
        </div>
    )
}
```

We can add the Layout component to the page like this:

```
const Page1 = () => {
    const user = useUser();
    if (!user) {
        return (
            <Layout>
                <div>Unauthenticated!</div>
            </Layout
        )
    }
    return (
        <Layout>
            <h1>Page 1</h1>
        </Layout>
    )
}
```

This way of handling layouts in Next.js applications is OK for some simple cases. However, it comes with some drawbacks, as described in the following list:

- If the Layout component tracks some internal state, it will lose it when the page changes
- The page will lose its scroll position
- Anything we want to return before the final return, we also need to wrap with Layout

For our application, we will use a better way to handle per-page layouts by attaching them to the page component. Let's see it in action in the following section.

## Attaching the layout to the page component and using it to wrap the entire component

To make this work, we need to first update the src/pages/_app.tsx file:

```
import { NextPage } from 'next';
import type { AppProps } from 'next/app';
import { ReactElement, ReactNode } from 'react';

import { AppProvider } from '@/providers/app';

type NextPageWithLayout = NextPage & {
  getLayout?: (page: ReactElement) => ReactNode;
};

type AppPropsWithLayout = AppProps & {
  Component: NextPageWithLayout;
};

const App = ({
  Component,
  pageProps,
}: AppPropsWithLayout) => {
  const getLayout =
    Component.getLayout ?? ((page) => page);

  const pageContent = getLayout(
    <Component {...pageProps} />
```

```
    );

  return <AppProvider>{pageContent}</AppProvider>;
};


export default App;
```

The page component expects the getLayout static property to be attached, which will be used to wrap the entire component when it is rendered in _app.tsx. Thanks to the reconciliation in React, all of the layout component states will persist when navigating between pages with the same layout.

We already have the layout components built and will just add them to our pages.

Now that we have everything prepared, let's build out our pages.

## Building the pages

Now that we are acquainted with how Next.js pages work and have prepared the Seo component and the layout setup, let's implement the pages for the application. We will be implementing the following pages:

- The public organization details page
- The public job details page
- The jobs page in the dashboard
- The job details page in the dashboard
- The create job page
- 404 page

### The public organization details page

The public organization details page is the page where any user can see all details about a given organization and a list of its jobs. Since it is a public page, we want to render it on the server for better SEO.

To create the page, let's create the src/pages/organizations/[organizationId]/index.tsx file, where organizationId refers to the dynamic ID of the organization, which will be used to retrieve the given organization.

Then, let's import all dependencies:

```
import { Heading, Stack } from '@chakra-ui/react';
import {
  GetServerSidePropsContext,
  InferGetServerSidePropsType,
} from 'next';
import { ReactElement } from 'react';

import { NotFound } from '@/components/not-found';
import { Seo } from '@/components/seo';
import { JobsList, Job } from '@/features/jobs';
import { OrganizationInfo } from '@/features/
  organizations';
import { PublicLayout } from '@/layouts/public-layout';
import {
  getJobs,
  getOrganization,
} from '@/testing/test-data';
```

Now, let's implement the page component:

```
type PublicOrganizationPageProps =
  InferGetServerSidePropsType<typeof getServerSideProps>;

const PublicOrganizationPage = ({
  organization,
  jobs,
}: PublicOrganizationPageProps) => {
  if (!organization) return <NotFound />;

  return (
    <>
      <Seo title={organization.name} />
      <Stack
        spacing="4"
        w="full"
```

```
          maxW="container.lg"
          mx="auto"
          mt="12"
          p="4"
       >
          <OrganizationInfo organization={organization} />
          <Heading size="md" my="6">
            Open Jobs
          </Heading>
          <JobsList
            jobs={jobs}
            organizationId={organization.id}
            type="public"
          />
        </Stack>
      </>
    );
};
```

The page component accepts `organization` and `jobs` as props. The props are passed to the page automatically by Next.js. What gets passed as props to a page component is determined by the return value of the `getServerSideProps` function, which is executed on the server and enables server-side rendering. We will see the implementation of it in a moment, but for now, let's wire up the layout:

```
PublicOrganizationPage.getLayout = function getLayout(
  page: ReactElement
) {
  return <PublicLayout>{page}</PublicLayout>;
};
```

This is how we will use layouts for our pages based on the setup we just configured. The `getLayout` function will wrap the page component, and the layouts will be applied. We can also nest multiple layouts if required, so this approach is very flexible.

Now, let's export our page, which must be exported as `default`:

```
export default PublicOrganizationPage;
```

And then, let's implement the `getServerSideProps` function:

```
export const getServerSideProps = async ({
  params,
}: GetServerSidePropsContext) => {
  const organizationId = params?.organizationId as string;

  const [organization, jobs] = await Promise.all([
    getOrganization(organizationId).catch(() => null),
    getJobs(organizationId).catch(() => [] as Job[]),
  ]);

  return {
    props: {
      organization,
      jobs,
    },
  };
};
```

We are extracting the organization's ID from `params` and using this to fetch the organization and its jobs, and then we return it as props, which will be passed to the page component. The `getServerSideProps` function must be exported as a named export.

One more thing to note is that currently, we are loading data using the utility functions that load our testing data since we don't have our API ready. In the following chapters, we will see how to create an actual API integration, but for now, this will allow us to build most of the UI for our pages.

Let's now open `http://localhost:3000/organizations/amYXmIyT9mD9GyO6CCr`:

**Test Org 1**

| Email | Phone Number |
|---|---|
| **org1@test.com** | **944-528-1711** |

Totam alias fuga enim esse ullam sit. Nisi animi ut at voluptatem odit nam ea. Et fuga consequatur similique asperiores non suscipit corrupti aperiam. Molestiae quae aut laborum soluta blanditiis cupiditate hic nobis provident.Et quae aut labore aut rerum. Nisi at autem. Enim ipsum enim consectetur sequi consequatur. Sint qui qui quam. Voluptas dignissimos rem et natus. Autem et mollitia hic suscipit illum placeat.Optio aut sit assumenda quo eius omnis sed non consequatur. Numquam perferendis ea sit rerum officia cupiditate aut itaque doloremque. Itaque alias est repellendus. Esse consectetur tenetur velit autem excepturi. Velit perspiciatis saepe dolorum fugiat. Adipisci odio porro quibusdam similique sunt temporibus ipsam.Dolor assumenda aut qui et in perferendis et. Possimus quam qui impedit. Nesciunt aliquid qui consequatur possimus eos velit deserunt magni qui. Nam accusantium libero corrupti.Nulla in ut sunt rerum voluptatem rerum voluptates. Quis expedita natus earum similique officiis rem. Possimus similique architecto ut ad ea quia laborum. Officia voluptatibus quos aliquid delectus. Est voluptates necessitatibus iure et provident iusto at voluptatem sit. Molestiae exercitationem repellat tempore. Id excepturi officiis iste ullam similique et hic sit. Quis et eaque quidem. Qui voluptas ea et rem recusandae suscipit voluptatem sit. Sint ut officiis nihil perferendis nihil quibusdam molestiae. Blanditiis nihil ab illo. Voluptatem mollitia officia aperiam. Esse voluptatum voluptatem nihil minima. Placeat itaque aut numquam. Quis nobis commodi voluptatum ipsum perspiciatis aut. Omnis nulla enim natus architecto in. Autem ab aperiam vitae ipsa quia. Adipisci deleniti voluptas ea nam nesciunt. Doloribus delectus modi et. Voluptatem qui sit eaque qui totam. In facilis excepturi et quae et ullam maiores et sit. Enim consequatur dolorem dolorem eum ullam rerum cum similique odit. Aut velit rem est id et tenetur ut. Velit sunt et velit odit qui mollitia aut harum aut. Cupiditate doloribus dicta reprehenderit aliquid consequatur eum voluptas veritatis. Ut corporis sed et magni consequatur voluptatem.

**Open Jobs**

| POSITION | DEPARTMENT | LOCATION | |
|---|---|---|---|
| Product Manager | Product | London | View |
| UI/UX Designer | Design | Belgrade | View |
| Software Engineer | Engineering | Berlin | View |

Figure 4.2 – The public organization details page

And there is our organization details page! Organizations can use this link to share info about their organizations and the list of their job postings.

The page is rendered on the server, meaning the page's content will be immediately available to the user.

To verify that, disable JavaScript in your browser and refresh the page.

You will notice that there is no difference. All the content is available even if JavaScript is disabled because all the markup is generated on the server and returned to the client.

## The public job details page

The public job details page is the page that shows all details about a given job and allows users to apply for it. It should also be available to all users, so we want to make it search-engine friendly. Therefore, we want to render its content on the server, just as we did with the organization page.

Let's start by creating `src/pages/organizations/[organizationId]/jobs/[jobId].tsx`, where `jobId` refers to the ID of the job.

Then, let's import all required dependencies:

```
import { Stack, Button } from '@chakra-ui/react';
import {
  GetServerSidePropsContext,
  InferGetServerSidePropsType,
} from 'next';
import { ReactElement } from 'react';

import { NotFound } from '@/components/not-found';
import { Seo } from '@/components/seo';
import { PublicJobInfo } from '@/features/jobs';
import { PublicLayout } from '@/layouts/public-layout';
import {
  getJob,
  getOrganization,
} from '@/testing/test-data';
```

Then, let's define our job page component:

```
type PublicJobPageProps = InferGetServerSidePropsType<
  typeof getServerSideProps
>;

export const PublicJobPage = ({
  job,
  organization,
}: PublicJobPageProps) => {
  const isInvalid =
    !job ||
    !organization ||
```

```
      organization.id !== job.organizationId;

  if (isInvalid) {
    return <NotFound />;
  }


  return (
    <>
      <Seo title={`${job.position} | ${job.location}`} />
      <Stack w="full">
        <PublicJobInfo job={job} />
        <Button
          bg="primary"
          color="primaryAccent"
          _hover={{
            opacity: '0.9',
          }}
          as="a"
          href={`mailto:${organization?.email}?subject=
            Application for ${job.position} position`}
          target="_blank"
        >
          Apply
        </Button>
      </Stack>
    </>
  );
};
```

As we did with the organization page, we are loading the job and the organization via getServerSideProps and rendering the content on the server.

Next, we can attach the layout of the page and export it:

```
PublicJobPage.getLayout = function getLayout(
  page: ReactElement
) {
  return <PublicLayout>{page}</PublicLayout>;
```

```
};


export default PublicJobPage;
```

And finally, let's create the getServerSideProps function and export it:

```
export const getServerSideProps = async ({
  params,
}: GetServerSidePropsContext) => {
  const organizationId = params?.organizationId as string;
  const jobId = params?.jobId as string;

  const [organization, job] = await Promise.all([
    getOrganization(organizationId).catch(() => null),
    getJob(jobId).catch(() => null),
  ]);

  return {
    props: {
      job,
      organization,
    },
  };
};
```

We are fetching the job and organization data, and we pass that as props to the page. The content is rendered on the server, so it will be available to the client immediately, just as it was on the organization details page.

To verify that everything works, let's open http://localhost:3000/organizations/amYXmIyT9mD9GyO6CCr/jobs/2LJ_sgmy_880G9WivH5Hf:

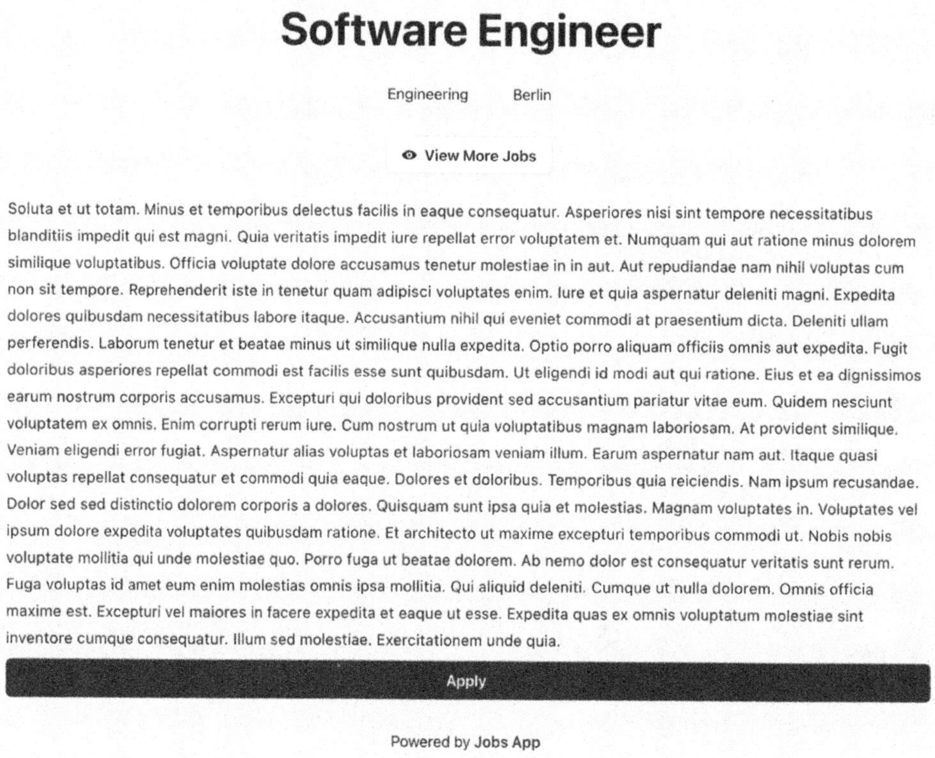

Figure 4.3 – The public job details page

It's nice to have the content immediately available on the client, so why wouldn't we render everything on the server?

Server-side rendering has a couple of drawbacks:

- More computing power for the server is required, which can affect server cost
- Long `getServerSideProps` execution time can block the entire application

That's why we want to use it only where it makes sense, such as public pages that should be search-engine friendly, and where their content might change more frequently.

For the dashboard pages, we will render the initial loading state on the server and then load and render data on the client.

## The jobs page in the dashboard

Let's create the `src/pages/dashboard/jobs/index.tsx` file.

Then, we can import all required dependencies:

```tsx
import { PlusSquareIcon } from '@chakra-ui/icons';
import { Heading, HStack } from '@chakra-ui/react';
import { ReactElement } from 'react';

import { Link } from '@/components/link';
import { Loading } from '@/components/loading';
import { Seo } from '@/components/seo';
import { JobsList } from '@/features/jobs';
import { DashboardLayout } from '@/layouts/dashboard-layout';
import { useJobs, useUser } from '@/testing/test-data';
```

Next, we can define and export the page component:

```tsx
const DashboardJobsPage = () => {
  const user = useUser();

  const jobs = useJobs(user.data?.organizationId ?? '');

  if (jobs.isLoading) return <Loading />;

  if (!user.data) return null;

  return (
    <>
      <Seo title="Jobs" />
      <HStack
        mb="8"
        align="center"
        justify="space-between"
      >
        <Heading>Jobs</Heading>
        <Link
          icon={<PlusSquareIcon />}
```

```
            variant="solid"
            href="/dashboard/jobs/create"
          >
            Create Job
          </Link>
        </HStack>
        <JobsList
          jobs={jobs.data || []}
          isLoading={jobs.isLoading}
          organizationId={user.data.organizationId}
          type="dashboard"
        />
      </>
    );
};


DashboardJobsPage.getLayout = function getLayout(
  page: ReactElement
) {
  return <DashboardLayout>{page}</DashboardLayout>;
};


export default DashboardJobsPage;
```

Notice how all data fetching happens in the component because we are doing it on the client.

To verify that everything works as expected, let's open http://localhost:3000/dashboard/jobs:

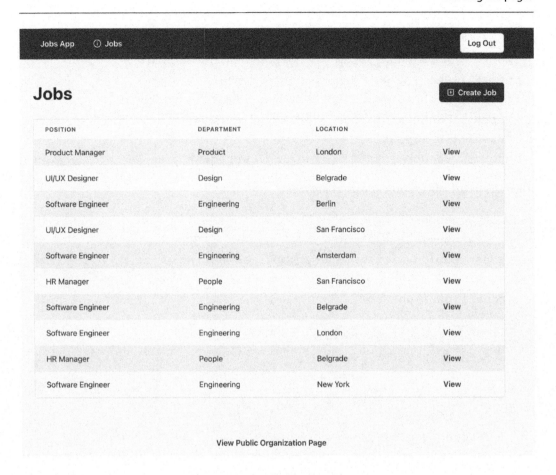

Figure 4.4 – The dashboard jobs page

And there it is! This page allows organization admins to have an overview of their organization's jobs.

## The job details page in the dashboard

The dashboard job details page will show all details about a given job in the dashboard.

To get started, let's create `src/pages/dashboard/jobs/[jobId].tsx`, where `jobId` refers to the dynamic ID of the job.

Then we can import all dependencies:

```
import { useRouter } from 'next/router';
import { ReactElement } from 'react';
```

```
import { Loading } from '@/components/loading';
import { NotFound } from '@/components/not-found';
import { Seo } from '@/components/seo';
import { DashboardJobInfo } from '@/features/jobs';
import { DashboardLayout } from '@/layouts/
  dashboard-layout';
import { useJob } from '@/testing/test-data';
```

Then let's define and export our page component:

```
const DashboardJobPage = () => {
  const router = useRouter();
  const jobId = router.query.jobId as string;

  const job = useJob(jobId);

  if (job.isLoading) {
    return <Loading />;
  }

  if (!job.data) {
    return <NotFound />;
  }

  return (
    <>
      <Seo
        title={`${job.data.position} | ${job.data.
          location}`}
      />
      <DashboardJobInfo job={job.data} />
    </>
  );
};

DashboardJobPage.getLayout = function getLayout(
  page: ReactElement
```

```
) {
  return <DashboardLayout>{page}</DashboardLayout>;
};


export default DashboardJobPage;
```

To verify that everything works as expected, let's open `http://localhost:3000/dashboard/jobs/wS6UeppUQoiXGTzAI6XrM`:

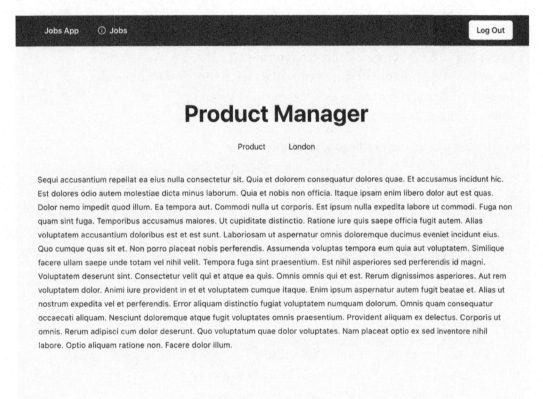

Figure 4.5 – The dashboard job details page

And this is our dashboard job details page. We can see basic details about a given job here.

## The create job page

The create job page is the page where we will render the form for creating jobs.

To get started, let's create `src/pages/dashboard/jobs/create.tsx`.

Then, let's import the required dependencies:

```
import { Heading } from '@chakra-ui/react';
import { useRouter } from 'next/router';
import { ReactElement } from 'react';

import { Seo } from '@/components/seo';
import { CreateJobForm } from '@/features/jobs';
import { DashboardLayout } from '@/layouts/
  dashboard-layout';
```

Then, we can create and export the page component:

```
const DashboardCreateJobPage = () => {
  const router = useRouter();

  const onSuccess = () => {
    router.push(`/dashboard/jobs`);
  };

  return (
    <>
      <Seo title="Create Job" />
      <Heading mb="8">Create Job</Heading>
      <CreateJobForm onSuccess={onSuccess} />
    </>
  );
};

DashboardCreateJobPage.getLayout = function getLayout(
  page: ReactElement
) {
  return <DashboardLayout>{page}</DashboardLayout>;
```

```
};

export default DashboardCreateJobPage;
```

To verify that everything works as expected, let's open `http://localhost:3000/dashboard/jobs/create`:

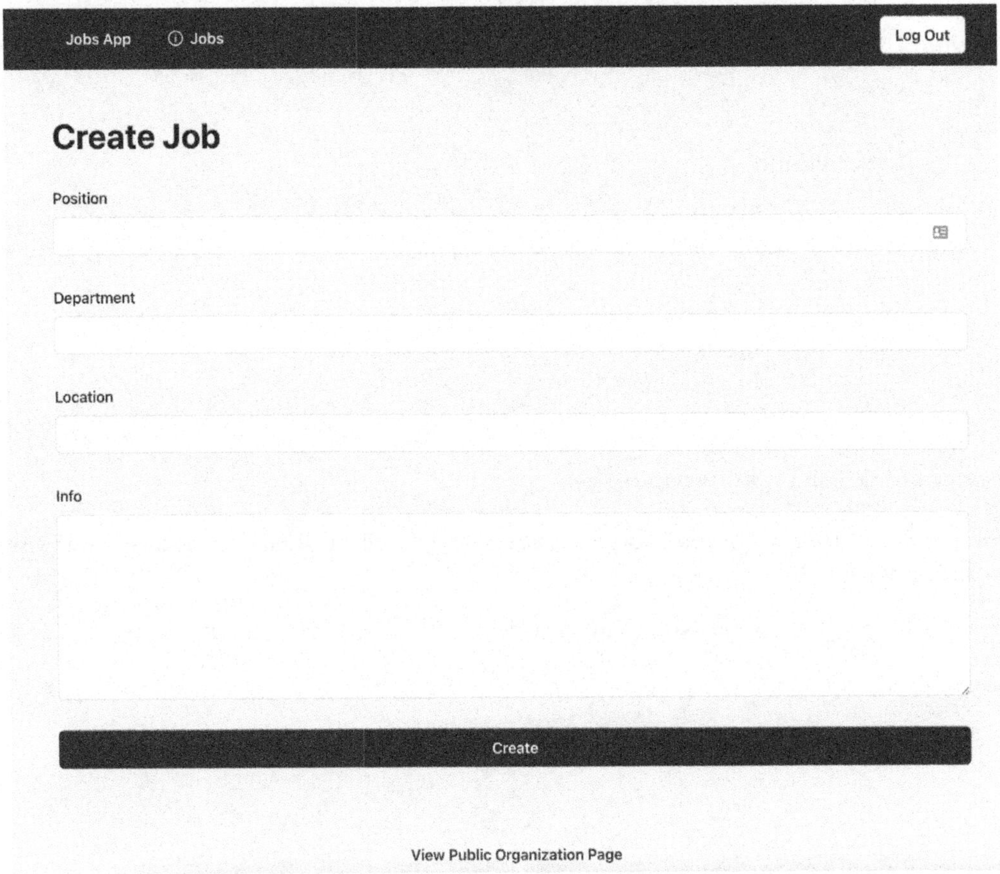

Figure 4.6 – The dashboard create job page

And there it is! For this chapter, we have just created the pages and will handle the data submission in the upcoming chapters.

## 404 page

If you tried to visit a page before we implemented it, you might have noticed a blank page. To let users know when they visit a non-existent page, we should create a custom 404 page.

Let's start by creating `src/pages/404.tsx` and add the following:

```tsx
import { Center } from '@chakra-ui/react';

import { Link } from '@/components/link';
import { NotFound } from '@/components/not-found';

const NotFoundPage = () => {
  return (
    <>
      <NotFound />
      <Center>
        <Link href="/">Home</Link>
      </Center>
    </>
  );
};

export default NotFoundPage;
```

The `404.tsx` file in the `pages` folder is a special page that will be displayed whenever a user visits an unknown page.

To verify that everything works as expected, let's visit `http://localhost:3000/non-existing-page`:

**Not Found**

Home

Figure 4.7 – 404 page

And there it is! We have a nice interface to return to the application if we end up on a missing page.

# Summary

In this chapter, our focus has been on building the pages of our application.

We started by looking at how routing works in Next.js. Then we covered the rendering strategies we will be using. After that, we built the SEO component, which injects content into the head of the page.

We then configured the layout system for our pages. At the end of the chapter, we built the pages for our application. To build the content for our pages, we used test data that was predefined. We used test data to render content on the pages, but we still need to make real API calls.

In the next chapter, we will learn how to mock the API endpoints, which we can use during development to make HTTP requests and fetch data as if we were consuming the real API.

# 5

# Mocking the API

In the previous chapter, we built the application pages that use test data. The UI of the pages is complete, but the pages are not functional yet. We are using the test data without making requests to the API.

In this chapter, we will learn what mocking is and why it is useful. We will learn how to mock the API endpoints with the msw library, a great tool that allows us to create mocked API endpoints that behave as real-world API endpoints.

We will also learn how to model the data of our application entities with the @mswjs/data library.

In this chapter, we will cover the following topics:

- Why is mocking useful?
- Introduction to MSW
- Configuring data models
- Configuring request handlers for API endpoints

By the end of this chapter, we will learn how to generate fully featured mocked APIs with data models set in place, which will make our code base less dependent on external APIs during development.

## Technical requirements

Before we get started, we need to set up our project. To be able to develop our project, we will need the following things installed on our computer:

- **Node.js** version 16 or above and **npm** version 8 or above

    There are multiple ways to install Node.js and npm. Here is a great article that goes into more detail: https://www.nodejsdesignpatterns.com/blog/5-ways-to-install-node-js.

- **Visual Studio Code (VS Code)** (optional) is currently the most popular editor/IDE for JavaScript/TypeScript, so we will be using it. It is open source, has great integration with TypeScript, and we can extend its features via extensions. It can be downloaded from here: `https://code.visualstudio.com/`.

The code files for this chapter can be found here: `https://github.com/PacktPublishing/React-Application-Architecture-for-Production`

The repository can be cloned locally with the following command:

```
git clone https://github.com/PacktPublishing/React-Application-Architecture-for-Production.git
```

Once the repository is cloned, we need to install the application's dependencies:

```
npm install
```

We can provide the environment variables using the following command:

```
cp .env.example .env
```

Once the dependencies have been installed, we need to select the right stage of the code base that matches this chapter. We can do that by executing the following command:

```
npm run stage:switch
```

This command will prompt us with a list of stages for each chapter:

```
? What stage do you want to switch to? (Use arrow
  keys)
> chapter-02
  chapter-03
  chapter-03-start
  chapter-04
  chapter-04-start
  chapter-05
  chapter-05-start
(Move up and down to reveal more choices)
```

This is the fifth chapter, so we can select `chapter-05-start` if we want to follow along, or `chapter-05` to see the final results of the chapter.

Once the chapter has been selected, all files required to follow along with the chapter will appear.

For more information about the setup details, check out the README.md file.

## Why is mocking useful?

**Mocking** is the process of simulating parts of the system, meaning they are not production-ready but fake versions that are useful for development and testing.

You may ask yourself, *Why do we want to bother with setting a mocked API?* There are several benefits of having the API mocked:

- **Independence of external services during development**: A web application usually consists of many different parts such as the frontend, the backend, external third-party APIs, and so on. When developing our frontends, we want to be as autonomous as possible without getting blocked by some parts of the system that are not functional. If the API of our application is broken or unfinished, we should still be able to proceed with developing the frontend part of the application.

- **Good for quick prototyping**: Mocked endpoints allow us to prototype the application quicker since they don't require any additional setup such as the backend server, database, and so on. Very useful for building **proofs of concept** (**POCs**) and **minimum viable product** (**MVP**) applications.

- **Offline development**: Having mocked API endpoints allows us to develop our application without an internet connection.

- **Testing**: We do not want to hit our real services while testing our frontends. That's where mocked APIs become useful. We can build and test the entire functionality as if we were building it against a real API and then switch to the real one when in production.

For testing our API endpoints, we will use the **Mock Service Worker** (**MSW**) library, a great tool that allows us to mock endpoints in a very elegant way.

## Introduction to MSW

**MSW** is a tool that allows us to create mocked APIs. It works as a service worker that intercepts any API request that has its mocked version defined. We can inspect the requests and responses in the **Network** tab of our browser the same way as if we were calling the real API.

To get a high-level overview of how it works, let's take a look at the diagram provided on their website:

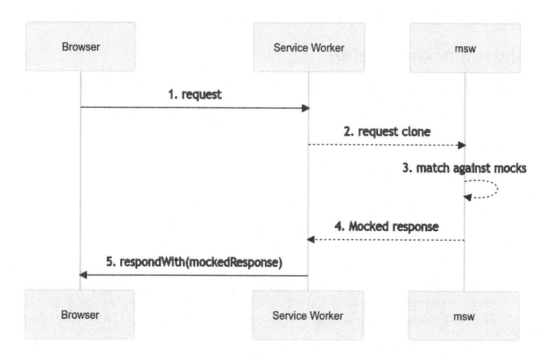

Figure 5.1 – MSW workflow diagram

One great thing about MSW is that our application will behave the same as if it were using a real API, and it's pretty trivial to switch to using the real API by turning mocked endpoints off and not intercepting requests.

Another great thing is that since the interception happens at the network level, we will still be able to inspect our requests in the **Network** tab of the browser dev tools.

## Configuration overview

We already have the MSW package installed as a dev dependency. The msw mocked API can be configured to work both in the browser and on the server.

### Browser

The *browser* version of the mocked API can be used for running mocked endpoints during the development of the application.

### Initialization

The first thing that needs to be done is to create a service worker. This can be done by executing the following command:

```
npx msw init public/ --save
```

The preceding command will create a service worker at `public/mockServiceWorker.js`, which will intercept our requests in the browser and modify the responses accordingly.

### Configuring the worker for the browser

We can now configure our worker to use the endpoints we will define in a couple of moments. Let's open the `src/testing/mocks/browser.ts` file and add the following:

```
import { setupWorker } from 'msw';

import { handlers } from './handlers';

export const worker = setupWorker(...handlers);
```

The preceding snippet will configure MSW to work with the provided handlers in the browser.

### *Server*

The *server* version is used mostly during running automated tests since our test runner works in the Node environment instead of the browser. The server version is also useful for API calls executed on the server, which we will have for our application during server-side rendering.

### Configuring MSW for the server

Let's open the `src/testing/mocks/server.ts` file and add the following:

```
import { setupServer } from 'msw/node';

import { handlers } from './handlers';

export const server = setupServer(...handlers);
```

The preceding snippet will apply the handlers to the server version of our mocks.

### Running MSW in the application

Now that we have configured MSW, we need to make it run in our application. To do that, let's open the src/testing/mocks/initialize.ts file and modify the initializeMocks function to the following:

```
import { IS_SERVER } from '@/config/constants';

const initializeMocks = () => {
  if (IS_SERVER) {
    const { server } = require('./server');
    server.listen();
  } else {
    const { worker } = require('./browser');
    worker.start();
  }
};


initializeMocks();
```

The initializeMocks function is in charge of calling the proper MSW setup based on the environment it is being called in. If it is executed on the server, it will run the server version. Otherwise, it will start the browser version.

Now, we need to integrate our mocks.

Let's create an src/lib/msw.tsx file and add the following:

```
import { MSWDevTools } from 'msw-devtools';
import { ReactNode } from 'react';

import { IS_DEVELOPMENT } from '@/config/constants';
import { db, handlers } from '@/testing/mocks';

export type MSWWrapperProps = {
  children: ReactNode;
};


require('@/testing/mocks/initialize');
```

```
export const MSWWrapper = ({
  children,
}: MSWWrapperProps) => {
  return (
    <>
      {IS_DEVELOPMENT && (
        <MSWDevTools db={db} handlers={handlers} />
      )}
      {children}
    </>
  );
};
```

Here we defined `MSWWrapper`, which is a component that will wrap our application and initialize MSW and the MSW dev tools into the wrapped application.

Now we can integrate it into our application by opening `src/pages/_app.tsx`.

We want to add new imports:

```
import dynamic from 'next/dynamic';
import { API_MOCKING } from '@/config/constants';
import { MSWWrapperProps } from '@/lib/msw';
```

Then, we want to load `MSWWrapper` dynamically:

```
const MSWWrapper = dynamic<MSWWrapperProps>(() =>
  import('@/lib/msw').then(({ MSWWrapper }) => MSWWrapper)
);
```

Finally, let's modify the `return` statement of our App component as follows:

```
return (
    <AppProvider>
      {API_MOCKING ? (
        <MSWWrapper>{pageContent}</MSWWrapper>
      ) : (
        pageContent
      )}
```

```
      </AppProvider>
  );
```

As you can see, we will load the `MSWWrapper` component and wrap the content of the page only if the mocks are enabled. We are doing this to exclude MSW-related code for the production version of the application, which uses the real API and does not need the redundant MSW-related code.

To verify that MSW is running, let's open the console. We should see something like this:

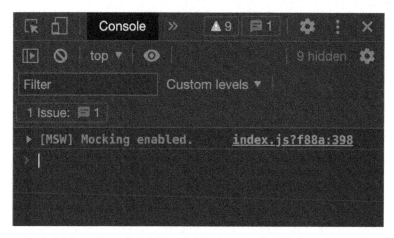

Figure 5.2 – MSW running in our application

Now that we have successfully installed and integrated MSW in our application, let's implement our first mocked endpoint.

## Writing our first handler

To define mocked endpoints, we need to create request handlers. Think of request handlers as functions that determine whether a request should be intercepted and modified by mocking their responses.

Let's create our first handler in the `src/testing/mocks/handlers/index.ts` file by adding the following:

```
import { rest } from 'msw';

import { API_URL } from '@/config/constants';

export const handlers = [
  rest.get(`${API_URL}/healthcheck`, (req, res, ctx) => {
    return res(
```

```
      ctx.status(200),
      ctx.json({ healthy: true })
    );
  }),
];
```

We are using the `rest` helper provided by `msw` to define our rest endpoints. We are using the `get` method, which accepts the path, and a callback, which will modify the response.

The handler callback will return a response with a status code of `200` and the response data set as `{ healthy: true }`.

To verify that our handler is working, let's open the dev tools in the bottom-right corner and then select the health check endpoint:

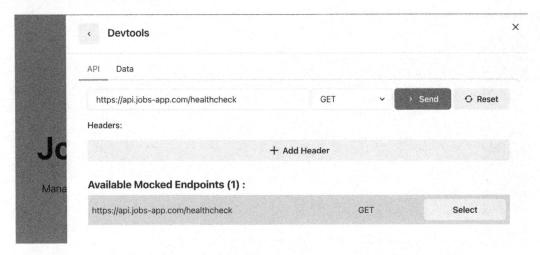

Figure 5.3 – Health check handler test selection

Sending the request should give us a response, as shown here:

Figure 5.4 – Health check handler test result

The **Devtools** widget is going to give us the ability to test our handlers without creating the UI in the application right away.

Now that we have MSW running properly in our application, it is time to create a data model for our application.

## Configuring data models

For data modeling our application, we will be using the data library from MSW, which is very useful and simple to use to manipulate the data in a similar way an **object-relational mapper (ORM)** on the backend would.

To make our request handlers functional, we could just hardcode the responses, but where is the fun in that? With MSW and its data library, we can build a mocked backend that is fully functional with the business logic included should we decide to implement it.

To configure our data models, let's open the `src/testing/mocks/db.ts` file and add the following:

```
import { factory, primaryKey } from '@mswjs/data';

import { uid } from '@/utils/uid';

const models = {
  user: {
    id: primaryKey(uid),
    createdAt: Date.now,
    email: String,
    password: String,
    organizationId: String,
  },
  organization: {
    id: primaryKey(uid),
    createdAt: Date.now,
    adminId: String,
    name: String,
    email: String,
    phone: String,
    info: String,
  },
  job: {
    id: primaryKey(uid),
    createdAt: Date.now,
    organizationId: String,
```

```
        position: String,
        info: String,
        location: String,
        department: String,
      },
  };


  export const db = factory(models);
```

We are importing the `factory` and `primaryKey` functions from the `@mswjs/data` package. The `primaryKey` function allows us to define primary keys in our mocked database, and the `factory` function creates an in-memory database that we can use for testing.

We can then access a bunch of different methods on each model that allow us to manipulate our data more easily, as follows:

```
db.job.findFirst
db.job.findMany
db.job.create
db.job.update
db.job.delete
```

It would also be great if we could pre-fill some data in the database so that we always had something to show in our application. To do that, we should seed the database.

Let's open the `src/testing/mocks/seed-db.ts` file and add the following:

```
import { db } from './db';
import { testData } from '../test-data';


export const seedDb = () => {
  const userCount = db.user.count();

  if (userCount > 0) return;
```

```
  testData.users.forEach((user) => db.user.create(user));

  testData.organizations.forEach((organization) =>
    db.organization.create(organization)
  );

  testData.jobs.forEach((job) => db.job.create(job));
};
```

The seedDb function will populate the database with test data.

Let's execute it after our mocked endpoints have been initialized. Open src/testing/mocks/ initialize.ts and call the function, as follows:

```
import { IS_SERVER } from '@/config/constants';

import { seedDb } from './seed-db';

const initializeMocks = () => {
  if (IS_SERVER) {
    const { server } = require('./server');
    server.listen();
  } else {
    const { worker } = require('./browser');
    worker.start();
  }
  seedDb();
};
initializeMocks();
```

To inspect the data in our database, we can open the **Data** tab in **Devtools**:

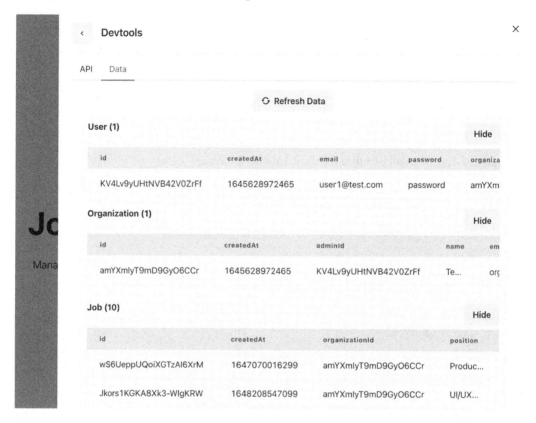

Figure 5.5 – Inspecting seeded data

Awesome! Now, we have our database pre-filled with some test data. We can now create request handlers, which will interact with the database and consume the data.

## Configuring request handlers for API endpoints

In this section, we will define handlers for our application. As already mentioned, a handler in MSW is a function that, if defined, will intercept any matching requests, and instead of sending the requests to the network, it will modify them and return the mocked response.

## API utils

Before getting started, let's take a quick look at the `src/testing/mocks/utils.ts` file, which includes some utilities we will be using for handling the business logic of our API handlers:

- `authenticate` accepts user credentials, and if they are valid, it will return the user from the database together with the authentication token.

- `getUser` returns a test user object.

- `requireAuth` returns the current user if the token in the cookie is available. It can optionally throw an error if the token does not exist.

Before getting started, let's include all handlers in the configuration. Open the `src/testing/mocks/handlers/index.ts` file and change it to the following:

```
import { rest } from 'msw';

import { API_URL } from '@/config/constants';

import { authHandlers } from './auth';
import { jobsHandlers } from './jobs';
import { organizationsHandlers } from './organizations';

export const handlers = [
  ...authHandlers,
  ...jobsHandlers,
  ...organizationsHandlers,
  rest.get(`${API_URL}/healthcheck`, (req, res, ctx) => {
    return res(
      ctx.status(200),
      ctx.json({ healthy: true })
    );
  }),
];
```

We are including all handlers we will define in each of the handlers' files and make them available to MSW.

Now, we can start working on the request handlers for our application.

## Auth handlers

For the `auth` feature, we will need the following endpoints:

- `POST /auth/login`
- `POST /auth/logout`
- `GET /auth/me`

The endpoints for `auth` will be defined in the `src/test/mocks/handlers/auth.ts` file.

Let's start by importing the dependencies:

```
import { rest } from 'msw';

import { API_URL } from '@/config/constants';

import {
  authenticate,
  requireAuth,
  AUTH_COOKIE,
} from '../utils';
```

Then, let's create a request handler for logging in:

```
const loginHandler = rest.post(
  `${API_URL}/auth/login`,
  async (req, res, ctx) => {
    const credentials = await req.json();
    const { user, jwt } = authenticate(credentials);

    return res(
      ctx.delay(300),
      ctx.cookie(AUTH_COOKIE, jwt, {
        path: '/',
        httpOnly: true,
      }),
      ctx.json({ user })
    );
```

```
    }
);
```

We are extracting the credentials and using them to get the user info and the token. Then, we attach the token to the cookie and return the user in the response with a 300 ms delay as the real API.

We are using the `httpOnly` cookie because it is safer since it is not accessible from the client.

Then, let's create a logout handler:

```
const logoutHandler = rest.post(
  `${API_URL}/auth/logout`,
  async (req, res, ctx) => {
    return res(
      ctx.delay(300),
      ctx.cookie(AUTH_COOKIE, '', {
        path: '/',
        httpOnly: true,
      }),
      ctx.json({ success: true })
    );
  }
);
```

The handler will just empty the cookie and return the response. Any subsequent requests to protected handlers will throw an error.

Finally, we have an endpoint for fetching the currently authenticated user:

```
const meHandler = rest.get(
  `${API_URL}/auth/me`,
  async (req, res, ctx) => {
    const user = requireAuth({ req, shouldThrow: false });

    return res(ctx.delay(300), ctx.json(user));
  }
);
```

The endpoint will extract the user from the token and return it in the response. In the end, we should export the handlers in order for them to be consumed by MSW:

```
export const authHandlers = [
  loginHandler,
  logoutHandler,
  meHandler,
];
```

## Jobs handlers

For the `jobs` feature, we will need the following endpoints:

- `GET /jobs`
- `GET /jobs/:jobId`
- `POST /jobs`

The endpoints for `jobs` will be defined in the `src/test/mocks/handlers/jobs.ts` file.

Let's start by importing the dependencies:

```
import { rest } from 'msw';

import { API_URL } from '@/config/constants';

import { db } from '../db';
import { requireAuth } from '../utils';
```

Then, let's implement a handler for fetching jobs:

```
const getJobsHandler = rest.get(
  `${API_URL}/jobs`,
  async (req, res, ctx) => {
    const organizationId = req.url.searchParams.get(
      'organizationId'
    ) as string;

    const jobs = db.job.findMany({
      where: {
        organizationId: {
```

```
        equals: organizationId,
      },
    },
  });

  return res(
    ctx.delay(300),
    ctx.status(200),
    ctx.json(jobs)
  );
  }
);
```

We are getting the organization ID from the search parameters and using that to get jobs for a given organization, which we return in the response.

Another endpoint we want to create is a job details endpoint. We can do that by creating the following handler:

```
const getJobHandler = rest.get(
  `${API_URL}/jobs/:jobId`,
  async (req, res, ctx) => {
    const jobId = req.params.jobId as string;

    const job = db.job.findFirst({
      where: {
        id: {
          equals: jobId,
        },
      },
    });

    if (!job) {
      return res(
        ctx.delay(300),
        ctx.status(404),
        ctx.json({ message: 'Not found!' })
      );
```

```
    }

    return res(
      ctx.delay(300),
      ctx.status(200),
      ctx.json(job)
    );
  }
);
```

We are getting the job ID from the URL parameters and using that to retrieve the given job from the database. If the job is not found, we return a 404 error. Otherwise, we return the job in the response.

Our application also needs an endpoint for creating jobs. We can create a handler for that, as follows:

```
const createJobHandler = rest.post(
  `${API_URL}/jobs`,
  async (req, res, ctx) => {
    const user = requireAuth({ req });

    const jobData = await req.json();

    const job = db.job.create({
      ...jobData,
      organizationId: user?.organizationId,
    });

    return res(
      ctx.delay(300),
      ctx.status(200),
      ctx.json(job)
    );
  }
);
```

We are first checking whether the user is authenticated since we don't want to allow creation for unauthenticated users. Then, we get the job data from the request and use that to create a new job, which we then return in the response.

Finally, we want to export the handlers to make them available for MSW:

```
export const jobsHandlers = [
  getJobsHandler,
  getJobHandler,
  createJobHandler,
];
```

## Organizations handlers

For the `organizations` feature, we will need the `GET /organizations/:organizationId` endpoint.

All handlers for this feature will be defined in the `src/test/mocks/handlers/organizations.ts` file.

Let's start by importing all required dependencies:

```
import { rest } from 'msw';

import { API_URL } from '@/config/constants';

import { db } from '../db';
```

Then, we can implement the endpoint for getting organization details by adding the following:

```
const getOrganizationHandler = rest.get(
  `${API_URL}/organizations/:organizationId`,
  (req, res, ctx) => {
    const organizationId = req.params
      .organizationId as string;

    const organization = db.organization.findFirst({
      where: {
        id: {
```

```
            equals: organizationId,
          },
        },
      });

      if (!organization) {
        return res(
          ctx.status(404),
          ctx.json({ message: 'Not found!' })
        );
      }

      return res(
        ctx.delay(300),
        ctx.status(200),
        ctx.json(organization)
      );
    }
  );
```

We are getting the organization ID from URL parameters and using that to retrieve the given organization. If it doesn't exist in the database, the handler will return a 404 error; otherwise, it will return the found organization.

In the end, we must export the handler:

```
export const organizationsHandlers = [
  getOrganizationHandler,
];
```

To verify that we have all handlers defined, we can visit **Devtools** again:

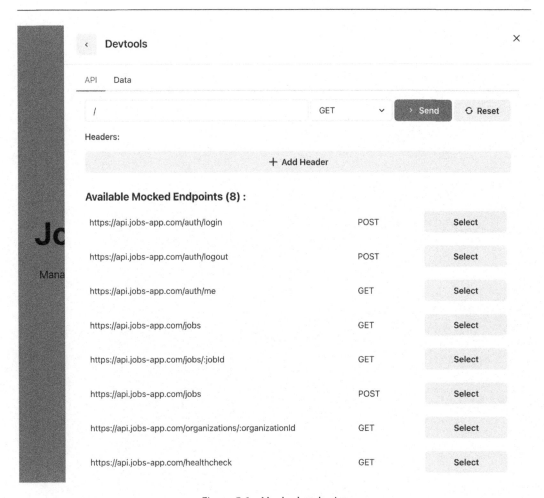

Figure 5.6 – Mocked endpoints

Great! Now, we have all the required handlers to make our application work as if it were consuming the real API. Play around with the handlers to make sure that everything works as expected. In the next chapter, we will integrate these endpoints into the application.

## Summary

In this chapter, we learned about mocking the API. We introduced the **MSW** library, which is a great tool for mocking APIs in an elegant way. It can work both in the browser and on the server. It is super useful for prototyping and testing the application during development.

In the next chapter, we will integrate the API layer of the application, which will consume the endpoints we just created.

# 6

# Integrating the API into the Application

In the previous chapter, we went through setting up the mocked API, which we will be consuming in our application.

In this chapter, we will be learning how to consume the API via the application.

When we say API, we mean the API backend server. We will learn how to fetch data from both the client and the server. For the HTTP client, we will be using **Axios**, and for handling fetched data, we will be using the **React Query** library, which allows us to handle API requests and responses in our React application.

In this chapter, we will cover the following topics:

- Configuring the API client
- Configuring React Query
- Creating the API layer for the features
- Using the API layer in the application

By the end of this chapter, we will know how to make our a
a clean and organized way.

# Technical requirements

Before we get started, we need to set up our project. To be able to develop our project, we will need the following things installed on our computer:

- **Node.js** version 16 or above and **npm** version 8 or above

  There are multiple ways to install Node.js and npm. Here is a great article that goes into more detail: `https://www.nodejsdesignpatterns.com/blog/5-ways-to-install-node-js`.

- **VSCode** (optional) is currently the most popular editor/IDE for JavaScript/TypeScript, so we will be using it. It is open source, has great integration with TypeScript, and we can extend its features via extensions. It can be downloaded from `https://code.visualstudio.com/`.

The code files for this chapter can be found here: `https://github.com/PacktPublishing/React-Application-Architecture-for-Production`

The repository can be cloned locally with the following command:

```
git clone https://github.com/PacktPublishing/React-Application-Architecture-for-Production.git
```

Once the repository has been cloned, we need to install the application's dependencies:

```
npm install
```

We can provide the environment variables using the following command:

```
cp .env.example .env
```

Once the dependencies have been installed, we need to select the right stage of the code base that matches this chapter. We can do that by executing the following command:

```
npm run stage:switch
```

This command will prompt us with a list of stages for each chapter:

```
? What stage do you want to switch to? (Use arrow
  ys)
    ter-02
    03
        start
```

```
chapter-05
chapter-05-start
(Move up and down to reveal more choices)
```

This is the sixth chapter, so we can select `chapter-06-start` if we want to follow along, or `chapter-06` to see the final results of this chapter.

Once the chapter has been selected, all the files required to follow along with this chapter will appear.

For more information about the setup details, check out the README.md file.

## Configuring the API client

For the API client of our application, we will be using Axios, a very popular library for handling HTTP requests. It is supported in both the browser and the server and has an API for creating instances, intercepting requests and responses, canceling requests, and so on.

Let's start by creating an instance of Axios, which will include some common things we want to be done on every request.

Create the `src/lib/api-client.ts` file and add the following:

```
import Axios from 'axios';

import { API_URL } from '@/config/constants';

export const apiClient = Axios.create({
  baseURL: API_URL,
  headers: {
    'Content-Type': 'application/json',
  },
});

apiClient.interceptors.response.use(
  (response) => {
    return response.data;
  },
  (error) => {
    const message =
      error.response?.data?.message || error.message;
```

```
        console.error(message);

        return Promise.reject(error);
    }
  );
```

Here, we have created an Axios instance where we define a common base URL and the headers we want to include in each request.

Then, we attached a response interceptor where we want to extract the data property from the response and return that to our client. We also defined the error interceptor where we want to log the error to the console.

Having an Axios instance configured is, however, not enough to handle requests in React components elegantly. We would still need to handle calling the API, waiting for the data to arrive, and storing it in a state. That's where React Query comes into play.

## Configuring React Query

React Query is a great library for handling async data and making it available in React components.

### Why React Query?

The main reason that React Query is a great option for handling the async remote state is the number of things it handles for us.

Imagine the following component, which loads some data from the API and displays it:

```
const loadData = () => Promise.resolve('data');

const DataComponent = () => {
  const [data, setData] = useState();
  const [error, setError] = useState();
  const [isLoading, setIsLoading] = useState();

  useEffect(() => {
    setIsLoading(true);
    loadData()
      .then((data) => {
        setData(data);
      })
```

```
      .catch((error) => {
        setError(error);
      })
      .finally(() => {
        setIsLoading(false);
      });
  }, []);

  if (isLoading) return <div>Loading</div>;
  if (error) return <div>{error}</div>;

  return <div>{data}</div>;
};
```

This is fine if we fetch data from an API only once, but in most cases, we need to fetch it from many different endpoints. We can see that there is a certain amount of boilerplate here:

- The same data, error, and isLoading pieces of state need to be defined
- Different pieces of state must be updated accordingly
- The data is thrown away as soon as we move away from the component

That's where React Query comes in. We can update our component to the following:

```
import { useQuery } from '@tanstack/react-query';

const loadData = () => Promise.resolve('data');

const DataComponent = () => {
  const {data, error, isLoading} = useQuery({
    queryFn: loadData,
    queryKey: ['data']
  })

  if (isLoading) return <div>Loading</div>;
  if (error) return <div>{error}</div>;

  return <div>{data}</div>;
};
```

Notice how the state handling is abstracted away from the consumer. We do not need to worry about storing the data, or handling loading and error states; everything is handled by React Query. Another benefit of React Query is its caching mechanism. For every query, we need to provide a corresponding query key that will be used to store the data in the cache.

This also helps with the deduplication of requests. If we called the same query from multiple places, it would make sure the API requests happen only once.

## Configuring React Query

Now, back to our application. We already have `react-query` installed. We just need to configure it for our application. The configuration needs a query client, which we can create in `src/lib/react-query.ts` and add the following:

```
import { QueryClient } from '@tanstack/react-query';

export const queryClient = new QueryClient({
  defaultOptions: {
    queries: {
      retry: false,
      refetchOnWindowFocus: false,
      useErrorBoundary: true,
    },
  },
});
```

React Query comes with a default configuration that we can override during the query client creation. A full list of options can be found in the documentation.

Now that we have created our query client, we must include it in the provider. Let's head to `src/providers/app.tsx` and replace the content with the following:

```
import {
  ChakraProvider,
  GlobalStyle,
} from '@chakra-ui/react';
import { QueryClientProvider } from '@tanstack/
  react-query';
import { ReactQueryDevtools } from '@tanstack/
  react-query-devtools';
import { ReactNode } from 'react';
```

```
import { ErrorBoundary } from 'react-error-boundary';

import { theme } from '@/config/theme';
import { queryClient } from '@/lib/react-query';

type AppProviderProps = {
  children: ReactNode;
};

export const AppProvider = ({
  children,
}: AppProviderProps) => {
  return (
    <ChakraProvider theme={theme}>
      <ErrorBoundary
        fallback={<div>Something went wrong!</div>}
        onError={console.error}
      >
        <GlobalStyle />
        <QueryClientProvider client={queryClient}>
          <ReactQueryDevtools initialIsOpen={false} />
          {children}
        </QueryClientProvider>
      </ErrorBoundary>
    </ChakraProvider>
  );
};
```

Here, we are importing and adding `QueryClientProvider`, which will make the query client and its configuration available for queries and mutations. Notice how we are passing our query client instance as the `client` prop.

We are also adding `ReactQueryDevtools`, which is a widget that allows us to inspect all queries. It only works in development, and that is very useful for debugging.

Now that our `react-query` setup is in place, we can start implementing the API layer for the features.

# Defining the API layer for the features

The API layer will be defined in the api folder of every feature. An API request can be either a query or a mutation. A query describes requests that only fetch data. A mutation describes an API call that mutates data on the server.

For every API request, we will have a file that includes and exports an API request definition function and a hook for consuming the request inside React. For the request definition functions, we will be using the API client we just created with Axios, and for the hooks, we will be using the hooks from React Query.

We'll learn how to implement it in action in the following sections.

## Jobs

For the jobs feature, we have three API calls:

- GET /jobs
- GET /jobs/:jobId
- POST /jobs

### Get jobs

Let's start with the API call that fetches jobs. To define it in our application, let's create the src/features/jobs/api/get-jobs.ts file and add the following:

```
import { useQuery } from '@tanstack/react-query';
import { apiClient } from '@/lib/api-client';
import { Job } from '../types';

type GetJobsOptions = {
  params: {
    organizationId: string | undefined;
  };
};

export const getJobs = ({
  params,
}: GetJobsOptions): Promise<Job[]> => {
  return apiClient.get('/jobs', {
    params,
```

```
    });
  };


export const useJobs = ({ params }: GetJobsOptions) => {
  const { data, isFetching, isFetched } = useQuery({
    queryKey: ['jobs', params],
    queryFn: () => getJobs({ params }),
    enabled: !!params.organizationId,
    initialData: [],
  });

  return {
    data,
    isLoading: isFetching && !isFetched,
  };
};
```

As we can see, there are a few things going on:

1.  We are defining the type for the request options. There, we can pass `organizationId` to specify the organization for which we want to get the jobs.

2.  We are defining the `getJobs` function, which is the request definition for getting jobs.

3.  We are defining the `useJobs` hook by using `useQuery` from `react-query`. The `useQuery` hook returns many different properties, but we want to expose only what is needed by the application. Notice how by using the `enabled` property, we are telling `useQuery` to run only if `organizationId` is provided. This means that the query will wait for `organizationId` to exist before fetching the data.

Since we will be using it outside the feature, let's make it available at `src/features/jobs/index.ts`:

```
export * from './api/get-jobs';
```

### Get job details

The get job request should be straightforward. Let's create the `src/features/jobs/api/get-job.ts` file and add the following:

```
import { useQuery } from '@tanstack/react-query';
```

```
import { apiClient } from '@/lib/api-client';

import { Job } from '../types';

type GetJobOptions = {
  jobId: string;
};

export const getJob = ({
  jobId,
}: GetJobOptions): Promise<Job> => {
  return apiClient.get(`/jobs/${jobId}`);
};

export const useJob = ({ jobId }: GetJobOptions) => {
  const { data, isLoading } = useQuery({
    queryKey: ['jobs', jobId],
    queryFn: () => getJob({ jobId }),
  });

  return { data, isLoading };
};
```

As we can see, we are defining and exporting the getJob function and the useJob query, which we will use in a moment.

We want to consume this API request outside the feature, so we have to make it available by re-exporting it from src/features/jobs/index.ts:

```
export * from './api/get-job';
```

### Create job

As we already mentioned, whenever we change something on the server, it should be considered a mutation. With that said, let's create the src/features/jobs/api/create-job.ts file and add the following:

```
import { useMutation } from '@tanstack/react-query';

import { apiClient } from '@/lib/api-client';
```

```
import { queryClient } from '@/lib/react-query';

import { Job, CreateJobData } from '../types';

type CreateJobOptions = {
  data: CreateJobData;
};

export const createJob = ({
  data,
}: CreateJobOptions): Promise<Job> => {
  return apiClient.post(`/jobs`, data);
};

type UseCreateJobOptions = {
  onSuccess?: (job: Job) => void;
};

export const useCreateJob = ({
  onSuccess,
}: UseCreateJobOptions = {}) => {
  const { mutate: submit, isLoading } = useMutation({
    mutationFn: createJob,
    onSuccess: (job) => {
      queryClient.invalidateQueries(['jobs']);
      onSuccess?.(job);
    },
  });

  return { submit, isLoading };
};
```

There are a few things going on here:

1.  We define the CreateJobOptions type of the API request. It will require a data object that contains all the fields that are required for creating a new job.

2.  We define the createJob function, which makes the request to the server.

3.  We define `UseCreateJobOptions`, which accepts an optional callback to call if the request succeeds. This may become useful whenever we want to show a notification, redirect the user, or do anything that is not directly related to the API request.

4.  We are defining the `useCreateJob` hook, which uses `useMutation` from `react-query`. As defined in the type, it accepts an optional `onSuccess` callback that gets called if the mutation succeeds.

5.  To create the mutation, we provide the `createJob` function as `mutationFn`.

6.  We define `onSuccess` of `useMutation`, where we invalidate all job queries once a new job is created. Invalidating queries means that we want to set them as invalid in the cache. If we need them again, we will have to fetch them from the API.

7.  We are reducing the API surface of the `useCreateJob` hook to things that are used by the application, so we are just exposing `submit` and `isLoading`. We can always expose more things in the future if we notice we need them.

We don't have to export this request from the `index.ts` file since it is used only within the `jobs` feature.

## Organizations

For the `organizations` feature, we have one API call:

*   `GET /organizations/:organizationId`

### *Get organization details*

Let's create `src/features/organizations/api/get-organization.ts` and add the following:

```
import { useQuery } from '@tanstack/react-query';

import { apiClient } from '@/lib/api-client';

import { Organization } from '../types';

type GetOrganizationOptions = {
  organizationId: string;
};

export const getOrganization = ({
  organizationId,
}: GetOrganizationOptions): Promise<Organization> => {
```

```
  return apiClient.get(
    `/organizations/${organizationId}`
  );
};

export const useOrganization = ({
  organizationId,
}: GetOrganizationOptions) => {
  const { data, isLoading } = useQuery({
    queryKey: ['organizations', organizationId],
    queryFn: () => getOrganization({ organizationId }),
  });

  return { data, isLoading };
};
```

Here, we are defining a query that will fetch the organization based on the `organizationId` property we pass.

Since this query will also be used outside the `organizations` feature, let's also re-export from `src/features/organizations/index.ts`:

```
export * from './api/get-organization';
```

Now that we have defined all our API requests, we can start consuming them in our application.

## Consuming the API in the application

To be able to build the UI without the API functionality, we used test data on our pages. Now, we want to replace it with the real queries and mutations that we just made for communicating with the API.

### Public organization

We need to replace a couple of things now.

Let's open `src/pages/organizations/[organizationId]/index.tsx` and remove the following:

```
import {
  getJobs,
```

```
    getOrganization,
  } from '@/testing/test-data';
```

Now, we must load the data from the API. We can do that by importing `getJobs` and `getOrganization` from corresponding `features`. Let's add the following:

```
import { JobsList, Job, getJobs } from '@/features/jobs';
import {
  getOrganization,
  OrganizationInfo,
} from '@/features/organizations';
```

The new API functions are a bit different, so we need to replace the following code:

```
const [organization, jobs] = await Promise.all([
  getOrganization(organizationId).catch(() => null),
  getJobs(organizationId).catch(() => [] as Job[]),
]);
```

We must replace it with the following:

```
const [organization, jobs] = await Promise.all([
  getOrganization({ organizationId }).catch(() => null),
  getJobs({
    params: {
      organizationId: organizationId,
    },
  }).catch(() => [] as Job[]),
]);
```

## Public job

The same process should be repeated for the public job page.

Let's open `src/pages/organizations/[organizationId]/jobs/[jobId].tsx` and remove the following:

```
import {
  getJob,
  getOrganization,
} from '@/testing/test-data';
```

Now, let's import `getJob` and `getOrganization` from the corresponding features:

```
import { getJob, PublicJobInfo } from '@/features/jobs';
import { getOrganization } from '@/features/organizations';
```

Then, inside `getServerSideProps`, we need to update the following:

```
const [organization, job] = await Promise.all([
  getOrganization({ organizationId }).catch(() => null),
  getJob({ jobId }).catch(() => null),
]);
```

## Dashboard jobs

For the dashboard jobs, the only thing we need to do is to update the imports so that we no longer load jobs from test data but from the API.

Let's import `useJobs` from the `jobs` feature instead of the test data by updating the following lines in `src/pages/dashboard/jobs/index.tsx`:

```
import { JobsList, useJobs } from '@/features/jobs';


import { useUser } from '@/testing/test-data';
```

We will still keep `useUser` from `test-data` for now; we will replace this in the next chapter.

Since the newly created `useJobs` hook is a bit different than the `test-data` one, we need to update the way it is being used, as follows:

```
const jobs = useJobs({
  params: {
    organizationId: user.data?.organizationId ?? '',
  },
});
```

## Dashboard job

The job details page in the dashboard is also very straightforward.

In `src/pages/dashboard/jobs/[jobId].tsx`, let's remove `useJob`, which was imported from `test-data`:

```
import { useJob } from '@/testing/test-data';
```

Now, let's import it from the jobs feature:

```
import {
  DashboardJobInfo,
  useJob,
} from '@/features/jobs';
```

Here, we need to update how useJob is consumed:

```
const job = useJob({ jobId });
```

## Create job

For the job creation, we will need to update the form, which, when submitted, will create a new job.

Currently, the form is not functional, so we need to add a couple of things.

Let's open src/features/jobs/components/create-job-form/create-job-form. tsx and replace the content with the following:

```
import { Box, Stack } from '@chakra-ui/react';
import { useForm } from 'react-hook-form';

import { Button } from '@/components/button';
import { InputField } from '@/components/form';

import { useCreateJob } from '../../api/create-job';
import { CreateJobData } from '../../types';

export type CreateJobFormProps = {
  onSuccess: () => void;
};

export const CreateJobForm = ({
  onSuccess,
}: CreateJobFormProps) => {
  const createJob = useCreateJob({ onSuccess });

  const { register, handleSubmit, formState } =
```

```
  useForm<CreateJobData>();

const onSubmit = (data: CreateJobData) => {
  createJob.submit({ data });
};

return (
  <Box w="full">
    <Stack
      as="form"
      onSubmit={handleSubmit(onSubmit)}
      w="full"
      spacing="8"
    >
      <InputField
        label="Position"
        {...register('position', {
          required: 'Required',
        })}
        error={formState.errors['position']}
      />
      <InputField
        label="Department"
        {...register('department', {
          required: 'Required',
        })}
        error={formState.errors['department']}
      />
      <InputField
        label="Location"
        {...register('location', {
          required: 'Required',
        })}
        error={formState.errors['location']}
      />
```

```
            <InputField
              type="textarea"
              label="Info"
              {...register('info', {
                required: 'Required',
              })}
              error={formState.errors['info']}
            />

            <Button
              isDisabled={createJob.isLoading}
              isLoading={createJob.isLoading}
              type="submit"
            >
              Create
            </Button>
          </Stack>
        </Box>
      );
    };
```

There are a few things worth mentioning in this component:

1.  We are using the `useForm` hook to handle the form's state.

2.  We are importing and using the `useCreateJob` API hook we previously defined to submit the request.

3.  When the mutation succeeds, the `onSuccess` callback is called.

---

**Note**

The *create job* form requires the user to be authenticated. Since we didn't implement the authentication system yet, you can use the MSW dev tools to authenticate with the test user to try the form submission.

---

## Summary

In this chapter, we learned how to make the application communicate with its API. First, we defined an API client that allows us to unify the API requests. Then, we introduced **React Query**, a library for handling asynchronous states. Using it reduces boilerplate and simplifies the code base significantly.

Finally, we declared the API requests, and then we integrated them into the application.

In the next chapter, we will learn how to create an authentication system for our application where only authenticated users will be able to visit the dashboard.

# 7

# Implementing User Authentication and Global Notifications

In the previous chapters, we configured the pages, created mocked APIs, and made the API calls from our application. However, the application still relies on test data when it comes to the authentication of the users in the admin dashboard.

In this chapter, we will build the application's authentication system, allowing users to authenticate and access protected resources in the admin dashboard. We will also be creating a toast notification system to provide feedback to users if an action happens that we want to notify them about.

In this chapter, we will cover the following topics:

- Implementing the authentication system

- Implementing notifications

By the end of the chapter, we will have learned how to authenticate users in our application and also how to handle the global application state with Zustand.

## Technical requirements

Before we get started, we need to set up the project. To be able to develop the project, you will need the following things installed on your computer:

- **Node.js** version 16 or above and **npm** version 8 or above.

  There are multiple ways to install Node.js and npm. Here is a great article that goes into more detail: `https://www.nodejsdesignpatterns.com/blog/5-ways-to-install-node-js`.

- **VSCode** (optional) is currently the most popular editor/IDE for JavaScript/TypeScript, so we will be using it. It is open source, has great integration with TypeScript, and you can extend its features via extensions. It can be downloaded from here: `https://code.visualstudio.com/`.

The code files for this chapter can be found here: `https://github.com/PacktPublishing/React-Application-Architecture-for-Production`.

The repository can be cloned locally with the following command:

```
git clone https://github.com/PacktPublishing/React-Application-
Architecture-for-Production.git
```

Once the repository is cloned, we need to install the application's dependencies:

```
npm install
```

We can provide the environment variables using the following command:

```
cp .env.example .env
```

Once the dependencies have been installed, we need to select the right stage of the code base that matches this chapter. We can do that by executing the following command:

```
npm run stage:switch
```

This command will prompt us with a list of stages for each chapter:

```
? What stage do you want to switch to? (Use arrow
 keys)
> chapter-02
  chapter-03
  chapter-03-start
  chapter-04
  chapter-04-start
  chapter-05
  chapter-05-start
(Move up and down to reveal more choices)
```

This is the seventh chapter, so you can select `chapter-07-start` if you want to follow along, or `chapter-07` to see the final results of the chapter.

Once the chapter has been selected, all files required to follow along with the chapter will appear.

For more information about the setup details, check out the `README.md` file.

# Implementing the authentication system

Authentication is the process of identifying who the user on a platform is. In our application, we need to identify users when they access the admin dashboard.

Before implementing the system, we should look closely at how it will work.

## Authentication system overview

We are going to authenticate the users with a token-based authentication system. That means the API will expect the user to send their authentication token with the request to access protected resources.

Let's take a look at the following diagram and the subsequent steps:

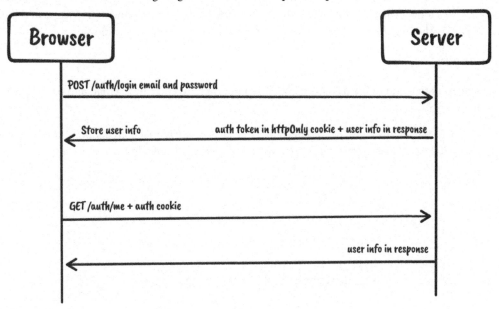

Figure 7.1 – Authentication system overview

The preceding diagram is explained as follows:

1.  The user submits the login form with the credentials by creating a request to the `/auth/login` endpoint.

2.  If the user exists and the credentials are valid, a response with the user data returns. In addition to the response data, we are also attaching an `httpOnly` cookie, which will be used from this point onward for authenticated requests.

3.  Whenever the user authenticates, we will store the user object from the response in react-query's cache and make it available to the application.

4.  Since the authentication is cookie-based with `httpOnly` cookies, we do not need to handle the authentication token on the frontend. Any subsequent requests will include the token automatically.

5.  Persisting user data on page refreshes will be handled by calling the `/auth/me` endpoint, which will fetch the user data and store it in the same react-query cache.

To implement this system, we need the following:

- Auth features (login, logout, and accessing the authenticated user)
- Protect resources that require the user to be authenticated

## Building authentication features

To build the authentication features, we already have the endpoints implemented.. We created them in *Chapter 5, Mocking the API*. Now we need to consume them in our application.

### Logging in

To allow users to log in to the dashboard, we'll require them to enter their email and password and submit the form.

To implement the login feature, we will need to make an API call to the login endpoint on the server. Let's create the `src/features/auth/api/login.ts` file and add the following:

```
import { useMutation } from '@tanstack/react-query';

import { apiClient } from '@/lib/api-client';
import { queryClient } from '@/lib/react-query';

import { AuthUser, LoginData } from '../types';

export const login = (
  data: LoginData
): Promise<{
  user: AuthUser;
}> => {
  return apiClient.post('/auth/login', data);
};

type UseLoginOptions = {
  onSuccess?: (user: AuthUser) => void;
```

```
};

export const useLogin = ({
  onSuccess,
}: UseLoginOptions = {}) => {
  const { mutate: submit, isLoading } = useMutation({
    mutationFn: login,
    onSuccess: ({ user }) => {
      queryClient.setQueryData(['auth-user'], user);
      onSuccess?.(user);
    },
  });

  return { submit, isLoading };
};
```

We are defining the API request and the API mutation hook, allowing us to call the API from our application.

Then, we can update the login form to make the API call. Let's modify `src/features/auth/components/login-form/login-form.tsx`.

First, let's import the `useLogin` hook:

```
import { useLogin } from '../../api/login';
```

Then, inside the `LoginForm` component body, we want to initialize the login mutation and submit it in the submit handler:

```
export const LoginForm = ({
  onSuccess,
}: LoginFormProps) => {
  const login = useLogin({ onSuccess });

  const { register, handleSubmit, formState } =
    useForm<LoginData>();

  const onSubmit = (data: LoginData) => {
    login.submit(data);
  };
```

```
        // rest of the component body
}
```

We should also indicate that the action is being submitted by disabling the **Submit** button:

```
<Button
  isLoading={login.isLoading}
  isDisabled={login.isLoading}
  type="submit"
>
  Log in
</Button>
```

When the form is submitted, it will call the login endpoint, which will authenticate the user if the credentials are valid.

### Logging out

To implement the logout feature, we need to call the logout endpoint, which will clear the auth cookie. Let's create the src/features/auth/api/logout.ts file and add the following:

```
import { useMutation } from '@tanstack/react-query';

import { apiClient } from '@/lib/api-client';
import { queryClient } from '@/lib/react-query';

export const logout = () => {
  return apiClient.post('/auth/logout');
};

type UseLogoutOptions = {
  onSuccess?: () => void;
};

export const useLogout = ({
  onSuccess,
}: UseLogoutOptions = {}) => {
  const { mutate: submit, isLoading } = useMutation({
    mutationFn: logout,
```

```
    onSuccess: () => {
      queryClient.clear();
      onSuccess?.();
    },
  });


  return { submit, isLoading };
};
```

We are defining the logout API request and the logout mutation.

Then, we can expose that from the auth feature by re-exporting it from the `src/features/auth/index.ts` file:

```
export * from './api/logout';
```

We want to use it when the user clicks the **Log Out** button, which will be located in the dashboard navbar. Let's go to the `src/layouts/dashboard-layout.tsx` file and import additional dependencies:

```
import { useRouter } from 'next/router';
import { useLogout } from '@/features/auth';
```

Then, in the `Navbar` component, let's use the `useLogout` hook:

```
const Navbar = () => {
  const router = useRouter();
  const logout = useLogout({
    onSuccess: () => router.push('/auth/login'),
  });


  // the rest of the component
};
```

Notice how we redirect the user to the login page when the logout action succeeds.

Let's finally wire the action to the logout button:

```
<Button
  isDisabled={logout.isLoading}
  isLoading={logout.isLoading}
  variant="outline"
```

```
  onClick={() => logout.submit()}
>
  Log Out
</Button>
```

Now, when the user clicks the **Log Out** button, the logout endpoint will be called, and then the user will be taken to the login page.

### Getting an authenticated user

To get started, let's create the `src/features/auth/api/get-auth-user.ts` file and add the following:

```
import { useQuery } from '@tanstack/react-query';

import { apiClient } from '@/lib/api-client';

import { AuthUser } from '../types';

export const getAuthUser = (): Promise<AuthUser> => {
  return apiClient.get('/auth/me');
};

export const useUser = () => {
  const { data, isLoading } = useQuery({
    queryKey: ['auth-user'],
    queryFn: () => getAuthUser(),
  });

  return { data, isLoading };
};
```

This endpoint will return information about the user currently logged in.

Then, we want to export it from the `src/features/auth/index.ts` file:

```
export * from './api/get-auth-user';
```

Back to the `src/layouts/dashboard-layout.tsx` file, we need the user data there.

Let's replace the `useUser` hook from the test data with the following:

```
import { useLogout, useUser } from '@/features/auth';
```

Another place where we need the user data is the dashboard jobs page. Let's open `src/pages/dashboard/jobs/index.tsx` and import the `useUser` hook:

```
import { useUser } from '@/features/auth';
```

## Protecting resources that require the user to be authenticated

What should happen if an unauthenticated user tries to view a protected resource? We want to ensure that any such attempt will redirect the user to the login page. To do that, we want to create a component that will wrap protected resources and let users view protected content only if they are authenticated.

The `Protected` component will fetch the user from the `/auth/me` endpoint, and if the user exists, it will allow the content to be shown. Otherwise, it will redirect the user to the login page.

The component has already been defined in the `src/features/auth/components/protected/protected.tsx` file, but it isn't doing much right now. Let's modify the file to the following:

```
import { Flex } from '@chakra-ui/react';
import { useRouter } from 'next/router';
import { ReactNode, useEffect } from 'react';

import { Loading } from '@/components/loading';

import { useUser } from '../../api/get-auth-user';

export type ProtectedProps = {
  children: ReactNode;
};

export const Protected = ({
  children,
}: ProtectedProps) => {
  const { replace, asPath } = useRouter();
  const user = useUser();

  useEffect(() => {
```

```
    if (!user.data && !user.isLoading) {
      replace(
        `/auth/login?redirect=${asPath}`,
        undefined,
        { shallow: true }
      );
    }
  }, [user, asPath, replace]);

  if (user.isLoading) {
    return (
      <Flex direction="column" justify="center" h="full">
        <Loading />
      </Flex>
    );
  }

  if (!user.data && !user.isLoading) return null;

  return <>{children}</>;
};
```

The component accepts children as props, meaning it will wrap nested content and decide whether it should be rendered.

We are accessing the user from the same useUser hook. Initially, while the data is being fetched, the component renders the Loading component. Once the data is fetched, we check in useEffect to see whether the user exists, and if it doesn't, we will redirect to the login page. Otherwise, we can render children as usual.

The Protected component is meant to be used in the dashboard. Since we already have a reusable layout for the dashboard, rather than wrapping every page with Protected, we can do that only once in the dashboard layout.

Let's open src/layouts/dashboard-layout.tsx and import the Protected component:

```
import { Protected } from '@/features/auth';
```

Then, in the JSX of the `DashboardLayout` component, let's wrap everything with `Protected` as follows:

```
export const DashboardLayout = ({
  children,
}: DashboardLayoutProps) => {
  const user = useUser();

  return (
    <Protected>
      <Box as="section" h="100vh" overflowY="auto">
        <Navbar />
        <Container as="main" maxW="container.lg" py="12">
          {children}
        </Container>
        <Box py="8" textAlign="center">
          <Link
            href={`/organizations/${user.data?.
              organizationId}`}
          >
            View Public Organization Page
          </Link>
        </Box>
      </Box>
    </Protected>
  );
};
```

If you try to visit the `http://localhost:3000/dashboard/jobs` page, you will be redirected to the login page.

Go ahead and try to log in with the existing credentials (email: user1@test.com; password: password). If everything is successful, you can access the dashboard with the data that belongs to the given user organization.

## Implementing notifications

Whenever something happens in the application, such as a successful form submission or a failed API request, we want to notify our users about it.

We will need to create a global store that will keep track of all notifications. We want it to be global because we want to show these notifications from anywhere in the application.

For handling global states, we will be using Zustand, a state management library that is lightweight and very simple to use.

## Creating the store

Let's open the `src/stores/notifications/notifications.ts` file and import the dependencies we will use:

```
import { createStore, useStore } from 'zustand';


import { uid } from '@/utils/uid';
```

Then, let's declare the notification types for the store:

```
export type NotificationType =
  | 'info'
  | 'warning'
  | 'success'
  | 'error';

export type Notification = {
  id: string;
  type: NotificationType;
  title: string;
  duration?: number;
  message?: string;
};

export type NotificationsStore = {
  notifications: Notification[];
  showNotification: (
    notification: Omit<Notification, 'id'>
  ) => void;
  dismissNotification: (id: string) => void;
};
```

The store will keep track of active notifications in an array. To show a notification, we need to call the `showNotification` method, and to dismiss it, we will call `dismissNotification`.

Let's create the store:

```
export const notificationsStore =
  createStore<NotificationsStore>((set, get) => ({
    notifications: [],
    showNotification: (notification) => {
      const id = uid();
      set((state) => ({
        notifications: [
          ...state.notifications,
          { id, ...notification },
        ],
      }));
      if (notification.duration) {
        setTimeout(() => {
          get().dismissNotification(id);
        }, notification.duration);
      }
    },
    dismissNotification: (id) => {
      set((state) => ({
        notifications: state.notifications.filter(
          (notification) => notification.id !== id
        ),
      }));
    },
  }));
```

To create the store, we use `createStore` from `zustand/vanilla` to make it more portable and testable. The function provides us with the `set` and `get` helpers, which allow us to modify and access the store, respectively.

Since we created the store using the vanilla approach, we need to make it compatible with React. We do that by exposing the store with the `useStore` hook provided by Zustand as follows:

```
export const useNotifications = () =>
  useStore(notificationsStore);
```

And that's the notification store. As you can see, it is very simple with minimal boilerplate.

Any time we need to access the store inside React components or hooks, we can use the `useNotifications` hook. Alternatively, if we want to access the store from a plain JavaScript function outside React, we can use `notificationStore` directly.

## Creating the UI

Now that we have the notifications store, we need to build a UI to display those notifications when active.

Let's open the `src/components/notifications/notifications.tsx` file and import the required dependencies:

```
import {
  Flex,
  Box,
  CloseButton,
  Stack,
  Text,
} from '@chakra-ui/react';

import {
  Notification,
  NotificationType,
  useNotifications,
} from '@/stores/notifications';
```

Then, let's create the `Notifications` component, which will display the notifications:

```
export const Notifications = () => {
  const { notifications, dismissNotification } =
    useNotifications();

  if (notifications.length < 1) return null;
```

```
    return (
      <Box
        as="section"
        p="4"
        position="fixed"
        top="12"
        right="0"
        zIndex="1"
      >
        <Flex gap="4" direction="column-reverse">
          {notifications.map((notification) => (
            <NotificationToast
              key={notification.id}
              notification={notification}
              onDismiss={dismissNotification}
            />
          ))}
        </Flex>
      </Box>
    );
};
```

We are accessing the notifications via the useNotifications hook, which provides us with access to the store.

As you can see, we are mapping through the active notifications. We render the NotificationToast component for each active notification and pass the notification object and the dismiss handler as props. Let's implement it by describing the variants and prop types:

```
const notificationVariants: Record<
  NotificationType,
  { color: string }
> = {
  info: {
    color: 'primary',
  },
  success: {
    color: 'green',
```

```
  },
  warning: {
    color: 'orange',
  },
  error: {
    color: 'red',
  },
};

type NotificationToastProps = {
  notification: Omit<Notification, 'duration'>;
  onDismiss: (id: string) => void;
};
```

Then, implement the NotificationToast component:

```
const NotificationToast = ({
  notification,
  onDismiss,
}: NotificationToastProps) => {
  const { id, type, title, message } = notification;

  return (
    <Box
      w={{ base: 'full', sm: 'md' }}
      boxShadow="md"
      bg="white"
      borderRadius="lg"
      {...notificationVariants[type]}
    >
      <Stack
        direction="row"
        p="4"
        spacing="3"
        justifyContent="space-between"
      >
        <Stack spacing="2.5">
```

```
            <Stack spacing="1">
              <Text fontSize="sm" fontWeight="medium">
                {title}
              </Text>
              {notification.message && (
                <Text fontSize="sm" color="muted">
                  {message}
                </Text>
              )}
            </Stack>
          </Stack>
          <CloseButton
            onClick={() => onDismiss(id)}
            transform="translateY(-6px)"
          />
        </Stack>
      </Box>
  );
};
```

Now that we have the notifications store and the UI created, it is time to integrate them into the application.

## Integrating and using notifications

To integrate notifications into the application, let's open the `src/providers/app.tsx` file and import the `Notifications` component:

```
import { Notifications } from '@/components/notifications';
```

Then, let's render the component in `AppProvider`:

```
export const AppProvider = ({
  children,
}: AppProviderProps) => {
  return (
    <ChakraProvider theme={theme}>
      <GlobalStyle />
      <Notifications />
      {/* rest of the code */}
```

```
        </ChakraProvider>
    );
};
```

Perfect! Now we are ready to start showing some notifications.

As mentioned, we can use the store both in the React world and outside it.

We will need to use it in a React component from the page for creating jobs. Any time we create a job successfully, we want to let the user know.

Let's open the `src/pages/dashboard/jobs/create.tsx` file and import the `useNotifications` hook:

```
import { useNotifications } from '@/stores/notifications';
```

Then, let's initialize the hook inside the `DashboardCreateJobPage` component body:

```
const { showNotification } = useNotifications();
```

Then, we can call `showNotification` in the `onSuccess` handler:

```
const onSuccess = () => {
  showNotification({
    type: 'success',
    title: 'Success',
    duration: 5000,
    message: 'Job Created!',
  });
  router.push(`/dashboard/jobs`);
};
```

We are showing a new success notification that will disappear after 5 seconds.

To see it in action, let's open `http://localhost:3000/dashboard/jobs/create` and submit the form. If the submission is successful, we should see something like this:

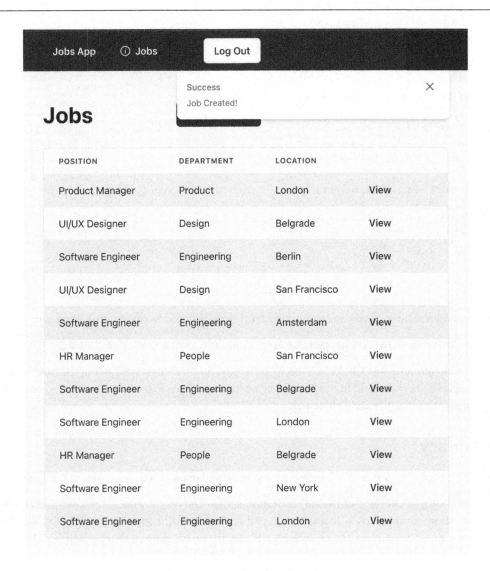

Figure 7.2 – Notifications in action

Perfect! Any time a job is created, the user will be notified about it.

Another place that we can utilize notifications is in API error handling. Whenever an API error happens, we want to let the user know something went wrong.

We can handle it on the API client level. Since Axios supports interceptors, and we already have them configured, we just need to modify the response error interceptor.

Let's open `src/lib/api-client.ts` and import the store:

```
import { notificationsStore } from '@/stores/notifications';
```

Then, in the response error interceptor, let's locate the following:

```
console.error(message);
```

We'll replace it with the following:

```
notificationsStore.getState().showNotification({
  type: 'error',
  title: 'Error',
  duration: 5000,
  message,
});
```

To access values and methods on a vanilla Zustand store, we need to call the `getState` method.

Any time an error on the API happens, an error notification will be shown to the user.

It's worth mentioning that Chakra UI has its own toast notification system out of the box, which is very simple to use and would fit our needs, but we made our own to learn how to manage the global application state in a nice and simple way.

## Summary

In this chapter, we learned how to handle authentication and manage the global state of the application.

We started with an overview of the authentication system and how it works. Then, we implemented authentication features such as login, logout, and getting the authenticated user info. We also built the `Protected` component, which controls whether the user is allowed to see a page based on their authentication status.

Then, we built a toast notification system where the user can trigger and display notifications from anywhere in the application. The main goal of building it was to introduce Zustand, a very simple and easy-to-use state management library for handling global application state.

In the next chapter, we will learn how to approach testing the application with unit, integration, and end-to-end tests.

# 8
# Testing

We have finally finished developing our application. Before we release it to production, we want to ensure that everything works as expected.

In this chapter, we will learn how to test our application by using different testing approaches. This will give us the confidence to refactor the application, build new features, and modify the existing ones without worrying about breaking the current application behavior.

We will be covering the following topics:

- Unit testing
- Integration testing
- End-to-end testing

By the end of this chapter, we will know how to test our application with different methods and tools.

## Technical requirements

Before we get started, we need to set up our project. To be able to develop our project, we will need the following things installed on our computer:

- **Node.js** version 16 or above and **npm** version 8 or above

  There are multiple ways to install Node.js and npm. Here is a great article that goes into more detail: `https://www.nodejsdesignpatterns.com/blog/5-ways-to-install-node-js`.

- **VSCode** (optional) is currently the most popular editor/IDE for JavaScript/TypeScript, so we will be using it. It is open source, has great integration with TypeScript, and we can extend its features via extensions. It can be downloaded from `https://code.visualstudio.com/`.

The code files for this chapter can be found here: `https://github.com/PacktPublishing/React-Application-Architecture-for-Production`.

The repository can be cloned locally with the following command:

```
git clone https://github.com/PacktPublishing/React-Application-Architecture-for-Production.git
```

Once the repository has been cloned, we need to install the application's dependencies:

```
npm install
```

We can provide the environment variables using the following command:

```
cp .env.example .env
```

Once the dependencies have been installed, we need to select the right stage of the code base that matches this chapter. We can do that by executing the following command:

```
npm run stage:switch
```

This command will prompt us with a list of stages for each chapter:

```
? What stage do you want to switch to? (Use arrow
  keys)
> chapter-02
  chapter-03
  chapter-03-start
  chapter-04
  chapter-04-start
  chapter-05
  chapter-05-start
(Move up and down to reveal more choices)
```

This is the eighth chapter, so we can select `chapter-08-start` if we want to follow along, or `chapter-08` to see the final results of this chapter.

Once the chapter has been selected, all the files required to follow along with this chapter will appear.

For more information about the setup details, check out the `README.md` file.

# Unit testing

Unit testing is a testing method where application units are tested in isolation without depending on other parts.

For unit testing, we will use Jest, which is the most popular framework for testing JavaScript applications.

In our application, we will unit test the notifications store.

Let's open the `src/stores/notifications/__tests__/notifications.test.ts` file and add the following:

```
import {
  notificationsStore,
  Notification,
} from '../notifications';

const notification = {
  id: '123',
  title: 'Hello World',
  type: 'info',
  message: 'This is a notification',
} as Notification;

describe('notifications store', () => {
  it('should show and dismiss notifications', () => {
    // 1
    expect(
      notificationsStore.getState().notifications.length
    ).toBe(0);

    // 2
    notificationsStore
      .getState()
      .showNotification(notification);

    expect(
      notificationsStore.getState().notifications
```

```
  ).toContainEqual(notification);

  // 3
  notificationsStore
    .getState()
    .dismissNotification(notification.id);

  expect(
    notificationsStore.getState().notifications
  ).not.toContainEqual(notification);
  });
});
```

The notifications test works as follows:

1.  We assert that the `notifications` array is initially empty.
2.  Then, we fire the `showNotification` action and test that the newly created notification exists in the `notifications` array.
3.  Finally, we call the `dismissNotification` function to dismiss the notification and make sure the notification is removed from the `notifications` array.

To run unit tests, we can execute the following command:

```
npm run test
```

Another use case for unit testing would be various utility functions and reusable components, including logic that could be tested in isolation. However, in our case, we will test our components mostly with integration tests, which we will see in the next section.

## Integration testing

Integration testing is a testing method where multiple parts of the application are tested together. Integration tests are generally more helpful than unit tests, and most application tests should be integration tests.

Integration tests are more valuable because they can give more confidence in our application since we are testing the functionality of different parts, the relationship between them, and how they communicate.

For integration testing, we will use Jest and the React Testing Library. This is a great approach to testing features of the application in the same way the user would use it.

In `src/testing/test-utils.ts`, we can define some utilities we can use in our tests. We should also re-export all utilities provided by the React Testing Library from here so that we can easily reach out to them whenever they are needed in our tests. Currently, in addition to all the functions provided by the React Testing Library, we are also exporting the following utilities:

- `appRender` is a function that calls the `render` function from the React Testing Library and adds `AppProvider` as a `wrapper`. We need this because, in our integration tests, our components rely on multiple dependencies defined in `AppProvider`, such as the React Query context, notifications, and more. Providing `AppProvider` as a `wrapper` will make it available when we render the component during testing.

- `checkTableValues` is a function that goes through all the cells in the table and compares each value with the corresponding value from the provided data, ensuring that all the information is displayed in the table.

- `waitForLoadingToFinish` is a function that waits for all loading spinners to disappear before we can proceed further with our tests. This is useful when we must wait for some data to be fetched before we can assert the values.

Another file worth mentioning is `src/testing/setup-tests.ts`, where we can configure different initialization and cleanup actions. In our case, it helps us initialize and reset the mocked API between tests.

We can split our integration tests by pages and test all the parts on each page. The idea is to perform integration tests on the following parts of our application:

- Dashboard jobs page
- Dashboard job page
- Create job page
- Login page
- Public job page
- Public organization page

## Dashboard jobs page

The functionality of the dashboard jobs page is based on the currently logged-in user. Here, we are fetching all the jobs of the user's organization and displaying them in the jobs table.

Let's start by opening the `src/__tests__/dashboard-jobs-page.test.tsx` file and adding the following:

```
import DashboardJobsPage from '@/pages/dashboard/jobs';
import { getUser } from '@/testing/mocks/utils';
```

```
import { testData } from '@/testing/test-data';
import {
  appRender,
  checkTableValues,
  screen,
  waitForLoadingToFinish,
} from '@/testing/test-utils';

// 1
jest.mock('@/features/auth', () => ({
  useUser: () => ({ data: getUser() }),
}));

describe('Dashboard Jobs Page', () => {
  it('should render the jobs list', async () => {
    // 2
    await appRender(<DashboardJobsPage />);

    // 3
    expect(screen.getByText(/jobs/i)).toBeInTheDocument();

    // 4
    await waitForLoadingToFinish();

    // 5
    checkTableValues({
      container: screen.getByTestId('jobs-list'),
      data: testData.jobs,
      columns: ['position', 'department', 'location'],
    });
  });
});
```

The test is working as follows:

1.  Since loading the jobs depends on the currently logged-in user, we need to mock the useUser hook to return the proper user object.

2.   Then, we render the page.

3.   Then, we make sure the jobs page's title is displayed on the page.

4.   To get the loaded jobs, we need to wait for them to finish loading.

5.   Finally, we assert the jobs values in the table.

## Dashboard job page

The functionality of the dashboard job page is that we want to load the job data and display it on the page.

Let's start by opening the `src/__tests__/dashboard-job-page.test.tsx` file and adding the following:

```
import DashboardJobPage from '@/pages/dashboard/jobs/
  [jobId]';
import { testData } from '@/testing/test-data';
import {
  appRender,
  screen,
  waitForLoadingToFinish,
} from '@/testing/test-utils';

const job = testData.jobs[0];

const router = {
  query: {
    jobId: job.id,
  },
};

// 1
jest.mock('next/router', () => ({
  useRouter: () => router,
}));

describe('Dashboard Job Page', () => {
  it('should render all the job details', async () => {
    // 2
```

```
  await appRender(<DashboardJobPage />);

  await waitForLoadingToFinish();

  const jobPosition = screen.getByRole('heading', {
    name: job.position,
  });

  const info = screen.getByText(job.info);

  // 3
  expect(jobPosition).toBeInTheDocument();
  expect(info).toBeInTheDocument();
  });
});
```

The test works as follows:

1. Since we are loading job data based on the `jobId` URL parameter, we need to mock the `useRouter` hook to return the proper job ID.

2. Then, we render the page and wait for the data to load by waiting for all loaders to disappear from the page.

3. Finally, we check that the job data is displayed on the page.

## Job creation page

The job creation page contains a form which, when submitted, calls the API endpoint that creates a new job on the backend. When the request succeeds, we redirect the user to the dashboard jobs page and show the notification about successful job creation.

Let's start by opening the `src/__tests__/dashboard-create-job-page.test.tsx` file and adding the following:

```
import DashboardCreateJobPage from '@/pages/dashboard/jobs/
  create';
import {
  appRender,
  screen,
  userEvent,
```

```
  waitFor,
} from '@/testing/test-utils';

const router = {
  push: jest.fn(),
};

// 1
jest.mock('next/router', () => ({
  useRouter: () => router,
}));

const jobData = {
  position: 'Software Engineer',
  location: 'London',
  department: 'Engineering',
  info: 'Lorem Ipsum',
};

describe('Dashboard Create Job Page', () => {
  it('should create a new job', async () => {
    // 2
    appRender(<DashboardCreateJobPage />);

    const positionInput = screen.getByRole('textbox', {
      name: /position/i,
    });

    const locationInput = screen.getByRole('textbox', {
      name: /location/i,
    });

    const departmentInput = screen.getByRole('textbox', {
      name: /department/i,
    });
```

```
    const infoInput = screen.getByRole('textbox', {
      name: /info/i,
    });

    const submitButton = screen.getByRole('button', {
      name: /create/i,
    });

    // 3
    userEvent.type(positionInput, jobData.position);
    userEvent.type(locationInput, jobData.location);
    userEvent.type(departmentInput, jobData.department);
    userEvent.type(infoInput, jobData.info);

    // 4
    userEvent.click(submitButton);

    // 5
    await waitFor(() =>
      expect(
        screen.getByText(/job created!/i)
      ).toBeInTheDocument()
    );
  });
});
```

The test works as follows:

1.  First, we need to mock the `useRouter` hook to contain the `push` method because it is used for navigating to the jobs page after the submission.

2.  Then, we render the page component.

3.  After that, we get all the inputs and insert values into them.

4.  Then, we submit the form by simulating the click event on the **Submit** button.

5.  After the submission, we need to wait for the **Job Created** notification to appear in the document.

## Public organization page

For the organization page, since we are rendering it on the server, we need to fetch the data on the server and display it on the page.

Let's start by opening the `src/__tests__/public-organization-page.test.tsx` file and defining the skeleton of the test suite, as follows:

```
import PublicOrganizationPage, {
  getServerSideProps,
} from '@/pages/organizations/[organizationId]';
import { testData } from '@/testing/test-data';
import {
  appRender,
  checkTableValues,
  screen,
} from '@/testing/test-utils';

const organization = testData.organizations[0];
const jobs = testData.jobs;

describe('Public Organization Page', () => {
  it('should use getServerSideProps that fetches and
    returns the proper data', async () => {

  });

  it('should render the organization details', async () => {

  });

  it('should render the not found message if the
    organization is not found', async () => {

  });
});
```

Now, we will focus on each test in the test suite.

First, we want to test that the `getServerSideProps` function fetches the right data and returns it as props, which will be provided on the page:

```
it('should use getServerSideProps that fetches and returns
  the proper data', async () => {
  const { props } = await getServerSideProps({
    params: {
      organizationId: organization.id,
    },
  } as any);

  expect(props.organization).toEqual(organization);
  expect(props.jobs).toEqual(jobs);
});
```

Here, we are calling the `getServerSideProps` function and asserting that the returned value contains the corresponding data.

In the second test, we want to verify that the data provided as props to the `PublicOrganizationPage` component is rendered properly:

```
it('should render the organization details', async () => {
  appRender(
    <PublicOrganizationPage
      organization={organization}
      jobs={jobs}
    />
  );

  expect(
    screen.getByRole('heading', {
      name: organization.name,
    })
  ).toBeInTheDocument();

  expect(
    screen.getByRole('heading', {
      name: organization.email,
    })
```

```
    ).toBeInTheDocument();

    expect(
      screen.getByRole('heading', {
        name: organization.phone,
      })
    ).toBeInTheDocument();

    checkTableValues({
      container: screen.getByTestId('jobs-list'),
      data: jobs,
      columns: ['position', 'department', 'location'],
    });
  });
```

In this test, we are rendering the page component and verifying that all the values are displayed on the page.

In the third test of the test suite, we want to assert that if the organization does not exist, we want to display the *not found* message:

```
it('should render the not found message if the organization is
not found', async () => {
  appRender(
    <PublicOrganizationPage
      organization={null}
      jobs={[]}
    />
  );

  const notFoundMessage = screen.getByRole('heading', {
    name: /not found/i,
  });

  expect(notFoundMessage).toBeInTheDocument();
});
```

Here, we are rendering the `PublicOrganizationPage` component with an organization value of `null`, and then verifying that the *not found* message should be in the document.

## Public job page

For the public job page, since we are rendering it on the server, we need to fetch the data on the server and display it on the page.

Let's start by opening the src/__tests__/public-job-page.test.tsx file and defining the skeleton for the tests:

```
import PublicJobPage, {
  getServerSideProps,
} from '@/pages/organizations/[organizationId]/jobs/[jobId]';
import { testData } from '@/testing/test-data';
import { appRender, screen } from '@/testing/test-utils';

const job = testData.jobs[0];
const organization = testData.organizations[0];

describe('Public Job Page', () => {
  it('should use getServerSideProps that fetches and
    returns the proper data', async () => {

  });

  it('should render the job details', async () => {

  });

  it('should render the not found message if the data does
    not exist', async () => {

  });
});
```

Now, we can focus on each test in the test suite.

First, we need to test the getServerSideProps function, which will fetch the data and return it via props to the page:

```
it('should use getServerSideProps that fetches and returns
  the proper data', async () => {
```

```
  const { props } = await getServerSideProps({
    params: {
      jobId: job.id,
      organizationId: organization.id,
    },
  } as any);

  expect(props.job).toEqual(job);
  expect(props.organization).toEqual(organization);
});
```

Here, we are calling getServerSideProps and asserting whetherthe return value matches the expected data.

Now, we can test PublicJobPage, where we want to ensure the provided data is displayed on the page:

```
it('should render the job details', async () => {
  appRender(
    <PublicJobPage
      organization={organization}
      job={job}
    />
  );

  const jobPosition = screen.getByRole('heading', {
    name: job.position,
  });

  const info = screen.getByText(job.info);

  expect(jobPosition).toBeInTheDocument();
  expect(info).toBeInTheDocument();
});
```

Here, we are rendering the page component and verifying that the given job's data is displayed on the page.

Finally, we want to assert the case where the data provided by getServerSideProps does not exist:

```
it('should render the not found message if the data does not
```

```
exist', async () => {
  const { rerender } = appRender(
    <PublicJobPage organization={null} job={null} />
  );

  const notFoundMessage = screen.getByRole('heading', {
    name: /not found/i,
  });

  expect(notFoundMessage).toBeInTheDocument();

  rerender(
    <PublicJobPage
      organization={organization}
      job={null}
    />
  );

  expect(notFoundMessage).toBeInTheDocument();

  rerender(
    <PublicJobPage organization={null} job={job} />
  );

  expect(notFoundMessage).toBeInTheDocument();

  rerender(
    <PublicJobPage
      organization={organization}
      job={{ ...job, organizationId: '123' }}
    />
  );

  expect(notFoundMessage).toBeInTheDocument();
});
```

Since there are several cases where the data can be considered invalid, we are using the `rerender` function, which can re-render the component with a different set of props. We assert that if the data is not found, the *not found* message is displayed on the page.

## Login page

The login page renders the login form, which, when submitted successfully, navigates the user to the dashboard.

Let's start by opening the src/__tests__/login-page.test.tsx file and adding the following:

```tsx
import LoginPage from '@/pages/auth/login';
import {
  appRender,
  screen,
  userEvent,
  waitFor,
} from '@/testing/test-utils';

// 1
const router = {
  replace: jest.fn(),
  query: {},
};

jest.mock('next/router', () => ({
  useRouter: () => router,
}));

describe('Login Page', () => {
  it('should login the user into the dashboard', async () => {
    // 2
    await appRender(<LoginPage />);

    const emailInput = screen.getByRole('textbox', {
      name: /email/i,
    });
```

```
    const passwordInput =
      screen.getByLabelText(/password/i);

    const submitButton = screen.getByRole('button', {
      name: /log in/i,
    });

    const credentials = {
      email: 'user1@test.com',
      password: 'password',
    };

    // 3
    userEvent.type(emailInput, credentials.email);
    userEvent.type(passwordInput, credentials.password);

    userEvent.click(submitButton);

    // 4
    await waitFor(() =>
      expect(router.replace).toHaveBeenCalledWith(
        '/dashboard/jobs'
      )
    );
  });
});
```

The test works as follows:

1.   We need to mock the useRouter hook because it is being used to navigate the user to the dashboard on successful submission.

2.   Next, we render the page.

3.   Then, we enter the credentials into the form and submit it.

4.   Finally, we expect the replace method on the router to be called with the /dashboard/jobs value, which should navigate the user to the dashboard if the login submission succeeds.

To run the integration tests, we can execute the following command:

```
npm run test
```

If we want to watch the changes in the test, we can execute the following command:

```
npm run test:watch
```

# End-to-end testing

End-to-end testing is a testing method where an application is tested as a complete entity. Usually, these tests consist of running the entire application with the frontend and the backend in an automated way and verifying that the entire system works.

In end-to-end tests, we usually want to test the happy path to confirm that everything works as expected.

To test our application end to end, we will be using Cypress, a very popular testing framework that works by executing the tests in a headless browser. This means that the tests will be running in a real browser environment. In addition to Cypress, since we have become familiar with the React Testing Library, we will use the Testing Library plugin for Cypress to interact with the page.

For our application, we want to test two flows of the application:

- Dashboard flow
- Public flow

## Dashboard flow

The dashboard flow is the flow for organization admins where we want to test authenticating the user and accessing and interacting with different parts of the dashboard.

Let's start by opening the `cypress/e2e/dashboard.cy.ts` file and adding the skeleton for our test:

```
import { testData } from '../../src/testing/test-data';

const user = testData.users[0];

const job = testData.jobs[0];

describe('dashboard', () => {
  it('should authenticate into the dashboard', () => {
```

```
  });

  it('should navigate to and visit the job details page', () =>
{

  });

  it('should create a new job', () => {

  });

  it('should log out from the dashboard', () => {

  });
});
```

Now, let's implement the tests.

First, we want to authenticate into the dashboard:

```
it('should authenticate into the dashboard', () => {
  cy.clearCookies();
  cy.clearLocalStorage();

  cy.visit('http://localhost:3000/dashboard/jobs');

  cy.wait(500);

  cy.url().should(
    'equal',
    'http://localhost:3000/auth/login?redirect=/dashboard/
      jobs'
  );

  cy.findByRole('textbox', {
    name: /email/i,
  }).type(user.email);
```

```
  cy.findByLabelText(/password/i).type(
    user.password.toLowerCase()
  );

  cy.findByRole('button', {
    name: /log in/i,
  }).click();

  cy.findByRole('heading', {
    name: /jobs/i,
  }).should('exist');
});
```

Here, we want to clear cookies and `localStorage`. Then, we must attempt to navigate to the dashboard; however, the application will redirect us to the login page. We must enter the credentials in the login form and submit it. After that, we will be redirected to the dashboard jobs page, where we can see the **Jobs** title.

Now that we are on the dashboard jobs page, we can proceed further by visiting the job details page:

```
it('should navigate to and visit the job details page', () => {
  cy.findByRole('row', {
    name: new RegExp(
      `${job.position} ${job.department} ${job.location}
        View`,
      'i'
    ),
  }).within(() => {
    cy.findByRole('link', {
      name: /view/i,
    }).click();
  });

  cy.findByRole('heading', {
    name: job.position,
  }).should('exist');

  cy.findByText(new RegExp(job.info, 'i')).should(
```

```
      'exist'
    );
  });
```

Here, we are clicking the **View** link of one of the jobs and navigating to the job details page, where we verify that the selected job data is being displayed on the page.

Now, let's test the job creation process:

```
it('should create a new job', () => {
  cy.go('back');

  cy.findByRole('link', {
    name: /create job/i,
  }).click();

  const jobData = {
    position: 'Software Engineer',
    location: 'London',
    department: 'Engineering',
    info: 'Lorem Ipsum',
  };

  cy.findByRole('textbox', {
    name: /position/i,
  }).type(jobData.position);
  cy.findByRole('textbox', {
    name: /department/i,
  }).type(jobData.department);
  cy.findByRole('textbox', {
    name: /location/i,
  }).type(jobData.location);
  cy.findByRole('textbox', {
    name: /info/i,
  }).type(jobData.info);

  cy.findByRole('button', {
    name: /create/i,
```

```
  }).click();

  cy.findByText(/job created!/i).should('exist');
});
```

Since we are on the job details page, we need to navigate back to the dashboard jobs page, where we can click on the **Create Job** link. This will take us to the create job page. Here, we fill in the form and submit it. When the submission succeeds, the **Job Created** notification should appear.

Now that we have tested at all the features of the dashboard, we can log out from the dashboard:

```
it('should log out from the dashboard', () => {
  cy.findByRole('button', {
    name: /log out/i,
  }).click();

  cy.wait(500);

  cy.url().should(
    'equal',
    'http://localhost:3000/auth/login'
  );
});
```

Clicking the **Log Out** button logs the user out and redirects them to the login page.

## Public flow

The public flow of the application is available for everyone who visits it.

Let's start by opening the `cypress/e2e/public.cy.ts` file and adding the skeleton of the test:

```
import { testData } from '../../src/testing/test-data';

const organization = testData.organizations[0];

const job = testData.jobs[0];

describe('public application flow', () => {
```

```
  it('should display the organization public page', () => {

  });

  it('should navigate to and display the public job details
    page', () => {

  });
});
```

Now, let's start implementing the tests.

First, we want to visit the organization page:

```
it('should display the organization public page', () => {
  cy.visit(
    `http://localhost:3000/organizations/${organization.id}`
  );

  cy.findByRole('heading', {
    name: organization.name,
  }).should('exist');

  cy.findByRole('heading', {
    name: organization.email,
  }).should('exist');

  cy.findByRole('heading', {
    name: organization.phone,
  }).should('exist');

  cy.findByText(
    new RegExp(organization.info, 'i')
  ).should('exist');
});
```

Here, we are visiting an organization details page and checking whether the data displayed there matches the organization.

Now that we are on the organization details page, we can view a job of the organization:

```
it('should navigate to and display the public job details
   page', () => {
   cy.findByTestId('jobs-list').should('exist');

   cy.findByRole('row', {
     name: new RegExp(
       `${job.position} ${job.department} ${job.location}
         View`,
       'i'
     ),
   }).within(() => {
     cy.findByRole('link', {
       name: /view/i,
     }).click();
   });

   cy.url().should(
     'equal',
     `http://localhost:3000/organizations/$
       {organization.id}/jobs/${job.id}`
   );

   cy.findByRole('heading', {
     name: job.position,
   }).should('exist');

   cy.findByText(new RegExp(job.info, 'i')).should(
     'exist'
   );
});
```

Here, we click the **View** link of a job, and then we navigate to the job details page, where we are asserting the job data.

To run end-to-end tests, we need to build the application first by running the following command:

```
npm run build
```

Then, we can start the tests by opening the browser:

```
npm run e2e
```

Alternatively, we can run the tests in headless mode since it is less resource-demanding, which is great for CI:

```
npm run e2e:headless
```

## Summary

In this chapter, we learned how to test our application, thus making it ready for production.

We started by learning about unit testing by implementing unit tests for our notifications store.

Since integration tests are much more valuable because they give more confidence that something is working properly, we used these tests to test the pages.

Finally, we created end-to-end tests for public and dashboard flows, where we tested the entire functionality of each flow.

In the next chapter, we will learn how to prepare and release our application to production. We will use these tests and integrate them within our CI/CD pipeline, where we will not allow the application to be released to production if any of the tests fail. This will keep our users more satisfied as there is less chance of bugs ending up in production.

# 9
# Configuring CI/CD for Testing and Deployment

Our application is finally ready to go to production and meet its first users. We have built its features and implemented all the required checks, such as linting, testing, and so on, which will give us the confidence that the application code is working correctly.

However, currently, all those checks must be executed on our local machine. Whenever we want to push a new feature to production, we need to run all the scripts and then redeploy the application manually, which is a very tedious process.

In this chapter, we will learn what CI/CD is. Then, we will learn what GitHub Actions is and what are the main parts of a GitHub Actions pipeline. We will then learn how to create a CI/CD pipeline that will automate the verification and deployment of the application to Vercel.

In this chapter, we will cover the following topics:

- What is CI/CD?
- Using GitHub Actions
- Configuring the pipeline for testing
- Configuring the pipeline for deploying to Vercel

By the end of this chapter, we will know how to configure the CI/CD pipeline with GitHub Actions and deploy the application to Vercel.

# Technical requirements

Before we get started, we need to set up our project. To be able to develop our project, we will need the following things installed on our computer:

- **Node.js** version 16 or above and **npm** version 8 or above.

- There are multiple ways to install Node.js and npm. Here is a great article that goes into more detail: `https://www.nodejsdesignpatterns.com/blog/5-ways-to-install-node-js`.

- **VSCode** (optional) is currently the most popular editor/IDE for JavaScript/TypeScript, so we will be using it. It is open source, has great integration with TypeScript, and we can extend its features via extensions. It can be downloaded from `https://code.visualstudio.com/`.

The code files for this chapter can be found here: `https://github.com/PacktPublishing/React-Application-Architecture-for-Production`.

The repository can be cloned locally with the following command:

```
git clone https://github.com/PacktPublishing/React-Application-
Architecture-for-Production.git
```

Once the repository has been cloned, we need to install the application's dependencies:

```
npm install
```

We can provide the environment variables using the following command:

```
cp .env.example .env
```

Once the dependencies have been installed, we need to select the right stage of the code base that matches this chapter. We can do that by executing the following command:

```
npm run stage:switch
```

This command will prompt us with a list of stages for each chapter:

```
? What stage do you want to switch to? (Use arrow
  keys)
> chapter-02
  chapter-03
  chapter-03-start
  chapter-04
  chapter-04-start
```

```
chapter-05
chapter-05-start
(Move up and down to reveal more choices)
```

This is the ninth chapter, so we can select `chapter-09-start` if we want to follow along, or `chapter-09` to see the final results of this chapter.

Once the chapter has been selected, all the files required to follow along with this chapter will appear.

For more information about the setup details, check out the `README.md` file.

## What is CI/CD?

**Continuous integration/continuous deployment (CI/CD)** is a method of delivering application changes to its users in an automated way. CI/CD should usually consist of the following parts:

- **Continuous Integration** is the automated process of verifying that the code has been built, tested, and merged into a repository
- **Continuous Delivery** means delivering changes to the repository
- **Continuous Deployment** means publishing the changes to the production server, where the changes are made available to the users

Now, let's think about how we could implement CI/CD for our application. We already have all the parts – we just need to put them together. The process would work like this:

- Run all code checks for the application (unit and integration testing, linting, type checking, format checking, and so on)
- Build the application and run end-to-end tests
- If both processes finish successfully, we can deploy our application

Here is how the process can be visualized:

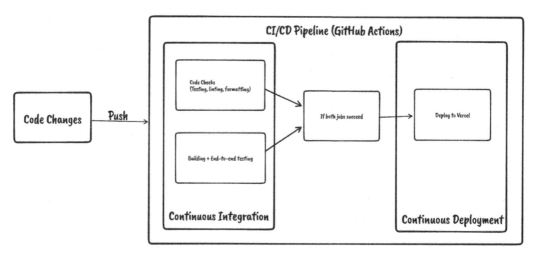

Figure 9.1 – Pipeline overview

This process will ensure our application is always in the best condition possible and that the changes get frequently and easily released to production. This is especially useful when working in larger teams where many changes are being introduced to the application on a daily basis.

To run the CI/CD pipeline, we need proper infrastructure. Since we keep the repository on GitHub, we can use GitHub Actions to handle CI/CD.

## Using GitHub Actions

**GitHub Actions** is a CI/CD tool that allows us to automate, build, test, and deploy pipelines. We can create workflows that run on a specific event in the repository.

To understand how it works, let's have a look at some of its components in the following sections.

### Workflows

A **workflow** is a process that can run one or more jobs. We can define them in YAML format within the `.github/workflows` folder. Workflows can be run when a specified event is triggered. We can also re-run workflows manually directly from GitHub. A repository can have as many workflows as we want.

## Events

An **event**, when fired, will cause the workflow to run. GitHub activities can trigger events, such as pushing to the repository or creating a pull request. Besides that, they can also be started on a schedule or via HTTP POST requests.

## Jobs

A **job** defines a series of steps that will be executed in a workflow. A step can be either an action or a script that can be executed.

A workflow can have many jobs that can run in parallel, or they can wait for dependent jobs to finish before starting.

## Actions

An **action** is an application that runs on GitHub Actions to perform a repetitive task. We can use already built actions available on `https://github.com/marketplace?type=actions`, or we can create our own. We will be using a couple of pre-made actions in our pipeline.

## Runners

A runner is a server that runs workflows when they get triggered. It can be hosted on GitHub, but it can also be self-hosted.

Now that we are familiar with the basics of GitHub Actions, we can start working on creating the workflow for our application.

Let's create the `.github/workflows/main.yml` file and the initial code:

```
name: CI/CD
on:
  - push
jobs:
# add jobs here
```

In the preceding code, we are providing the name of the workflow. If we omit it, the name will be assigned to the name of the workflow file. Here, we are defining the `push` event, which will cause the workflow to run whenever code changes get pushed to the repository.

We will define the jobs in the following sections.

For every job we define, we will provide the following:

```
name: Name of the job
runs-on: ubuntu-latest
```

These properties will be common for all the jobs:

- `name` sets the name of the running job

- `runs-on` sets the runner, which will run the job

Now that we learned what GitHub Actions is and what are the main parts of a pipeline, we can now start working on the pipelines for our application.

# Configuring the pipeline for testing

Our testing pipeline will consist of two jobs that should do the following:

- Run all code checks such as linting, type checking, unit and integration testing, and so on

- Build the application and run end-to-end tests

## Code checks job

The code checks job should work as shown in the following diagram:

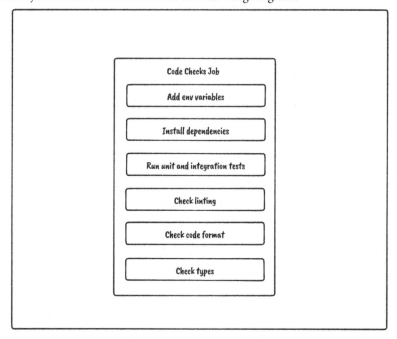

Figure 9.2 – Code checks job overview

As we can see, the job should be straightforward:

1. First, we need to provide environment variables to the application.

2. Then, we need to install the dependencies.

3. Next, we must run unit and integration tests.

4. Then, we must run linting.

5. After, we must check the code format.

6. Finally, we must run type checking.

Within jobs, let's add the job that runs these tasks:

```
jobs:
  code-checks:
    name: Code Checks
    runs-on: ubuntu-latest
    steps:
      - uses: actions/checkout@v3
      - uses: actions/setup-node@v3
        with:
          node-version: 16
      - run: mv .env.example .env
      - run: npm install
      - run: npm run test
      - run: npm run lint
      - run: npm run format:check
      - run: npm run types:check
```

There are a couple of things worth mentioning about the job:

- We use the actions/checkout@v3 action from the marketplace to allow the job to access the repository

- We use the actions/setup-node action to configure which node version to run

- We execute the scripts to verify that everything works as expected

## End-to-end testing job

Our second job related to testing is the end-to-end job, where we want to build the application and run the end-to-end tests we defined in the previous chapter.

It should work as shown in the following diagram:

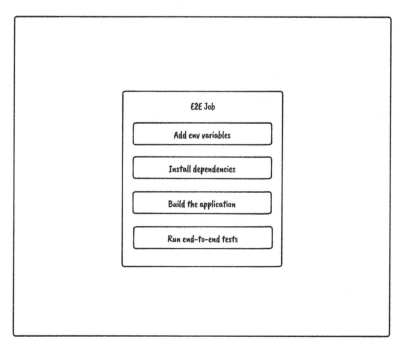

Figure 9.3 – E2E testing job

As we can see, the job will work as follows:

1.  First, we need to add the environment variables.

2.  Then, the dependencies for the applications need to be installed.

3.  Then, we need to create the production build of the application.

4.  Finally, the production code gets end-to-end tested.

To implement this job, let's add the following code:

```
jobs:
  # previous jobs
  e2e:
    name: E2E Tests
    runs-on: ubuntu-latest
    steps:
      - uses: actions/checkout@v3
      - run: mv .env.example .env
```

```
- uses: cypress-io/github-action@v4
  with:
    build: npm run build
    start: npm run start
```

There are a couple of things worth mentioning about the job:

- We use the `actions/checkout@v3` action to check out the repository.

- We use the `cypress-io/github-action@v4` action, which will abstract away the end-to-end testing. It will install all dependencies, build the application, and then start and run all Cypress tests.

Now that we configured the pipeline for running code checks such as linting, formatting, type checking, and testing, we can start working on deploying the application.

# Configuring the pipeline for deploying to Vercel

When our testing jobs finish, we want to deploy the application to Vercel. To start deploying to Vercel from GitHub Actions, we need to do a couple of things:

- Have a Vercel account

- Disable GitHub integration for Vercel

- Link the project to Vercel

- Provide environment variables to GitHub Actions

- Create the job that will deploy the application

## Having a Vercel account

Vercel is straightforward to get started with. Visit `https://vercel.com/signup` and create an account if you don't have one.

## Disabling GitHub integration for Vercel

**Vercel** is a platform that has excellent integration with GitHub out of the box. This means that whenever we push changes to the repository, a new version of the application will be deployed to Vercel automatically. However, in our case, we want to verify that our application works as expected before the deployment step so that we can perform this task from the CI/CD pipeline.

To do this, we need to disable GitHub integration in Vercel. This can be done by creating the `vercel.json` file with the following content:

```
{
  "version": 2,
  "github": {
    "enabled": false
  }
}
```

## Linking the project to Vercel

Since we have disabled GitHub integration, we need to link the project in Vercel to our repository. This can be done by using the Vercel CLI.

Let's execute the following command:

```
npx vercel
```

The CLI will ask us a series of questions, as follows:

```
? Set up and deploy "~/web/project-name"? [Y/n] y
? Which scope do you want to deploy to? org-name
? Link to existing project? [y/N] n
? What's your project's name? project-name
? In which directory is your code located? ./
```

Once the CLI process finishes, the `.vercel` folder will be generated. It is a folder that should never be tracked by the repository. Inside the `.vercel/project.json` file, we will find our project credentials, as follows:

```
{"orgId":"example_org_id","projectId":"example_project_id"}
```

We will need to provide these values to GitHub Actions in a few moments.

## Providing environment variables to GitHub Actions

For our pipeline, we need a couple of environment variables:

- `VERCEL_ORG_ID`, which we can get from the `.vercel/project.json` file
- `VERCEL_PROJECT_ID`, which we can also get from the `.vercel/project.json` file
- `VERCEL_TOKEN` which we can get from `https://vercel.com/account/tokens`

Once we have these values, we can add them to GitHub Actions for our project:

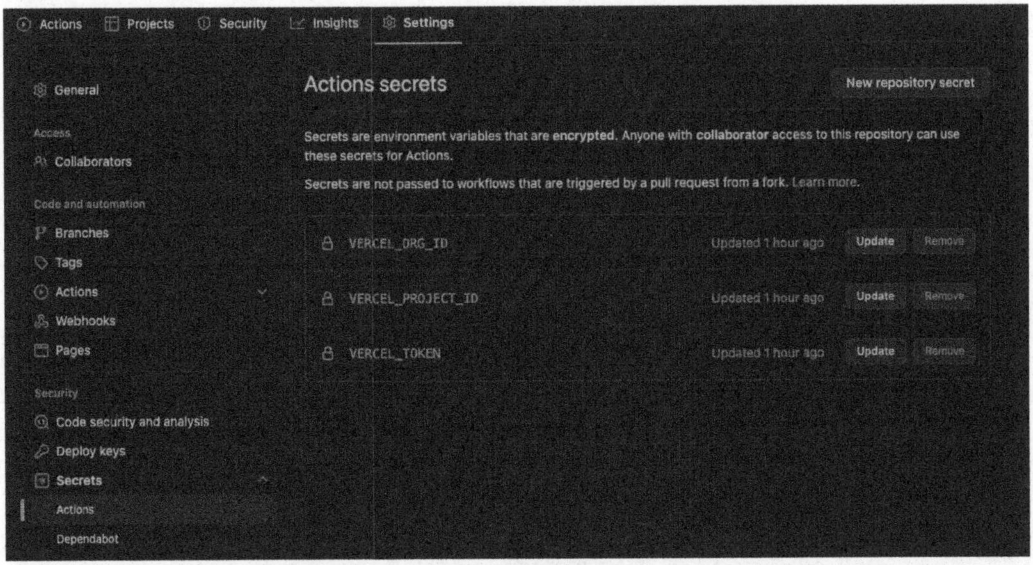

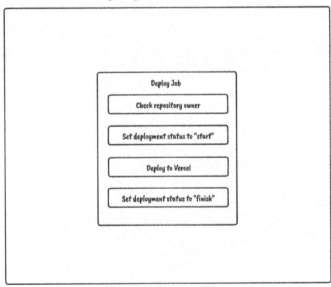

Figure 9.4 – Adding environment variables to GitHub Actions

## Creating the job that will deploy the application

Now that everything has been set, we can start working on the job that will do all the work. We can see how it should work in the following diagram:

Figure 9.5 – Deploy job overview

As we can see, it will go through a couple of steps:

1.  Check the repository owner since we do not want to deploy if the workflow is triggered from a repository fork.

2.  Set the deployment status to *start*.

3.  Deploy to Vercel.

4.  Set the deployment status to *finish*.

Let's add the `deploy` job to the workflow file, below the other jobs we defined previously:

```
jobs:
  # previous jobs
  deploy:
    name: Deploy To Vercel
    runs-on: ubuntu-latest
    needs: [code-checks, e2e]
    if: github.repository_owner == 'my-username'
    permissions:
      contents: read
      deployments: write
    steps:
      - name: start deployment
        uses: bobheadxi/deployments@v1
        id: deployment
        with:
          step: start
          token: ${{ secrets.GITHUB_TOKEN }}
          env: ${{ fromJSON('["Production", "Preview"]')
            [github.ref != 'refs/heads/master'] }}
      - uses: actions/checkout@v3
      - run: mv .env.example .env
      - uses: amondnet/vercel-action@v25
        with:
          vercel-token: ${{ secrets.VERCEL_TOKEN }}
          vercel-args: ${{ fromJSON('["--prod", ""]')
            [github.ref != 'refs/heads/master'] }}
          vercel-org-id: ${{ secrets.VERCEL_ORG_ID}}
```

```
          vercel-project-id: ${{ secrets.
            VERCEL_PROJECT_ID}}
          scope: ${{ secrets.VERCEL_ORG_ID}}
          working-directory: ./
      - name: update deployment status
        uses: bobheadxi/deployments@v1
        if: always()
        with:
          step: finish
          token: ${{ secrets.GITHUB_TOKEN }}
          status: ${{ job.status }}
          env: ${{ steps.deployment.outputs.env }}
          deployment_id: ${{ steps.deployment.outputs.
            deployment_id }}
```

There are a couple of things worth mentioning about the job:

- We set this job to depend on the previous two by adding needs: [code-checks, e2e]. This means that this job will wait until those jobs complete successfully before starting. If some of those jobs fail, this job will never run.

- With if: github.repository_owner == 'my-username', we check if the repository owner is the owner of the project. This check should prevent repository forks from deploying the application.

- We are using the bobheadxi/deployments@v1 action before and after the deploying task to update the deployment status in GitHub.

- We are using the amondnet/vercel-action@v25 action to deploy to Vercel. Depending on which branch got updated, it will be deployed either to a preview or production environment.

Our pipeline should look like this:

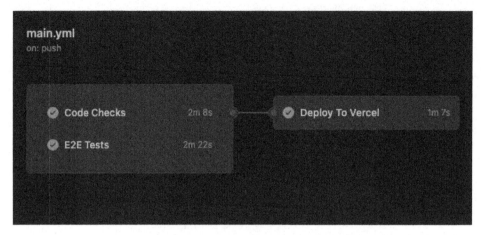

Figure 9.6 – Pipeline

We can track the deployment status of each environment in the bottom-right corner of the repository page:

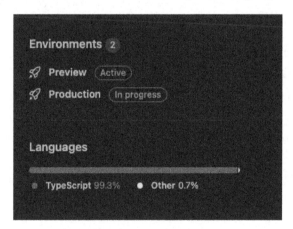

Figure 9.7 – Deployment statuses

Awesome! Our application is now in production and available for users. Configuring the pipeline might take a bit more effort initially, but it saves a lot of time in the long run as we don't have to worry about all these steps. They all just got automated.

# Summary

In this chapter, we learned that a CI/CD pipeline is a process that allows the automation of code changes and delivery. We also got introduced to GitHub Actions and the parts that allow us to create the CI/CD pipeline to automate testing and deploying our application.

After that, we defined three jobs for the workflow. With these jobs, we automated the process of running all the required checks, tests, and deployments. Finally, we learned how to deploy to Vercel from the CI/CD pipeline and deliver the application to the users.

This concludes the MVP version of our application. In the next chapter, we will cover some of the potential features and improvements we can make to the application.

# 10
# Going Beyond

Our application is finally in production. It might be getting some users as we speak. However, as with every piece of software, our application may never be fully completed. There is always room for improvement, and since the application we built is just an MVP, there are a lot of potential improvements worth mentioning.

In this chapter, we will be covering some of the most important improvements from both feature and technical perspectives. These topics might give us some ideas on extending and improving the existing application.

In this chapter, we will be covering the following topics:

- Feature improvements
- Technical improvements
- Appendix

By the end of this chapter, we will have covered some features we can add to the existing application to make it more complete. We will also mention some topics that were not covered in this book but are worth exploring on your own.

## Feature improvements

Since our application is at the MVP stage at the moment, there are many potential improvements from the user's perspective that would make the application more usable.

### Jobs feature improvements

The jobs feature is the most important feature of this app. There are several improvements we can implement to make the application better:

- Updating jobs
- Adding jobs in a draft state

- Deleting jobs
- Adding/updating jobs information with markdown/the *WYSIWYG* editor

## Updating jobs

Right now, our application only supports job creation. What happens when we want to change some information about the given job posting? It would be great if we could edit job data after it's been created.

Here is how we can do that:

- Create the *update* endpoint handler at `PATCH /jobs/:jobId`, which will update the data in the database
- Create the *update job* page at `/dashboard/jobs/:jobId/update`, which is where the update form should be
- Create the *update* form with all the fields that we want to be able to update for a job
- Upon successful submission, we should invalidate the job query so that its data gets refetched

## Adding jobs in a draft state

Currently, when we create a job for our organization, it will become immediately available to the public. However, it would be great if we could extend its functionality so that we can choose when we want to publish job postings to the public.

This can be done by doing the following:

- Extending the job model with the `status` property.
- Setting the `status` value to `draft` or `published`.
- When submitting the job creation form, the newly created job will initially have a `status` of `draft`.
- Then, we could update the status of the job via the *update* form, where we send the desired status as a value. Another way we could do this would be to expose a separate endpoint that would only update the status of the job.

## Deleting jobs

Most of the time, job positions get closed. In that case, no one wants a job posting that is no longer relevant, so it might be a good idea to allow organization admins to delete jobs they don't find relevant anymore.

This can be done in two ways:

- Having a *Delete* endpoint that will handle deleting the job from the database. Clicking on a button would send the request and, on a successful request, redirect the user to the jobs list.

- Extending the `status` property, which could now have an additional `archived` or `deleted` value. This method is called **soft delete** because we are not deleting the entry from the database, but from the application's perspective, it looks as if it was deleted. Archiving job postings might be useful for tracking different stats from previous hires.

### *Adding/updating jobs information with markdown/the WYSIWYG editor*

Currently, the job information is filled with a `textarea` input field, which is convenient for plain text values. However, the admin's ability to add as much information as possible is limited to text only.

It would be great if we could allow admins to add things, such as different headers, lists, links, and so on, to the job information so that the job posting provides as much information as possible.

The solution would be to replace the `textarea` input field with a rich text editor, which would allow us to add more than just text. Just make sure that you sanitize the inputs before submitting them to keep the application as safe as possible.

## Organization improvements

Currently, there is no way for the organization admin to update the organization's information. The organization should be able to change any of the information at any time.

To make this possible, we can do the following:

- Create the endpoint for updating the organization at `PATCH / organizations/:organizationId`

- Create a page at `/dashboard/organization/update` where we can have the update form

## Adding job applications

One more thing we can improve is the ability to add job applications.

Currently, there is no mechanism to apply to jobs directly in the application. When the user clicks the **Apply** button, the email client is opened with the correctly set subject. Then, the user would send an email to the organization's email address, and that would be the entire flow.

To take it to the next level, we can create another entity called *Application* that will be submitted when the user applies for a job. This approach will allow admins to track job applications for their organizations.

Let's rethink what the data model of the application will look like with this new feature:

**Application**

| Field Name | Field Type |
| --- | --- |
| id | string |
| createdAt | string |
| jobId | string |
| fullName | string |
| email | string |
| phone | string |
| report | string |
| status | string |
| message | string |

**User**

| Field Name | Field Type |
| --- | --- |
| id | string |
| createdAt | string |
| email | string |
| password | string |
| organizationId | string |

**Organization**

| Field Name | Field Type |
| --- | --- |
| id | string |
| createdAt | string |
| adminId | string |
| name | string |
| email | string |
| phone | string |
| info | string |

**Job**

| Field Name | Field Type |
| --- | --- |
| id | string |
| createdAt | string |
| organizationId | string |
| position | string |
| info | string |
| location | string |
| department | string |

Figure 10.1 – Applications in the data model

As we can see, an application should contain some basic information about the candidate, a message, a report from the interviewer, and so on.

Once the data model has been updated, we can build the applications feature, which will handle all things related. This would include things such as the following:

- Endpoints for creating and browsing applications.
- Pages on the dashboard where the admins can browse through all the applications. They can be defined at `/dashboard/applications` and `/dashboard/applications/:applicationId` for the listing and details pages, respectively.

## Filtering and paginating lists of data

Displaying lists of data in tables is fine, but what happens when the number of entries starts to grow significantly? It is not very optimal to load all the entries in one go because not all entries might be needed in the first place.

To optimize data lists, we can add support for filtering and paginating data. This will help users narrow down the search results to what they need. Both filtering and paginating should happen on the server.

Tracking current filter and pagination values should be handled by URL parameters. This will make it easy for the application to deep link the search results for any further usage.

## Adding user registration

This one is pretty straightforward. Until now, we have relied on test data, which had one test user that we used to sign in to the dashboard. However, there is no way to register new users. If we want to make this application usable by more than one organization, we should add this functionality. This can be implemented by doing the following:

- Creating the registration endpoint at POST `/auth/register`, which would take the required data from a form and create a user and its corresponding organization in the database

- Create the registration page at `/auth/register`, where there is the registration form which, when submitted, calls the registration endpoint

# Technical improvements

Our application is in good shape, but several things should be kept in mind in case the application starts growing. Let's take a look.

## Server-side rendering and caching

There are several improvements we can make to further optimize how the public pages are rendered on the server.

Currently, we are rendering the pages on each request, which is good if the data changes frequently; otherwise, it might increase the loading time and server costs because rendering on the server is a compute-intensive operation.

Fortunately, Next.js supports another rendering strategy called **Incremental Static Regeneration**.

It works as follows:

1. *User1* requests a page.
2. The server returns the cached version of the page and returns it.

3.  During that request, Next.js is triggered to regenerate the same page with the latest data.

4.  *User2* requests a page.

5.  The server returns the new version of the page.

If we take our public job details page as an example, it will work as follows.

First, we would need to use `getStaticPaths` to generate all the paths for all the jobs:

```
export const getStaticPaths = async () => {
  const jobs = await getJobs();

  const paths = jobs.map((job) => ({
    params: { jobId: job.id }
  }));

  return { paths, fallback: true };
}
```

This will generate a list of paths for all the jobs that exist in the database. The key thing here is the `fallback` property, which will make Next.js not return the 404 page but try to generate a new one.

We must also replace `getServerSideProps` with `getStaticProps`, which would look something like this:

```
export const getStaticProps = async ({
  params,
}: GetStaticPropsContext) => {
  const jobId = params?.jobId as string;

  const job = await getJob({ jobId });

  return {
    props: {
      job
    },
    revalidate: 60,
  };
};
```

Notice how we can add the `revalidate` property to the `return` value. This will force the page to revalidate after 60 seconds.

Since jobs and organizations' data don't change very frequently, this rendering strategy sounds more optimal in the long run, especially once the number of requests starts to grow.

It makes for a good compromise between the performance and freshness of the data.

## React Query hydration for SSR

Currently, we are using React Query for handling data fetching on the client, but data fetching on the server is being handled without it. We are just fetching the data and passing and rendering it on the page. This is fine if we don't have many levels of components, but there is a better way to do this.

React Query supports two ways of fetching data on the server and passing it to the client:

- Fetching the data on the server and then passing it as `initialData` to the query
- Prefetching on the server, dehydrating the cache, and rehydrating it on the client

The first option is good for smaller apps where there is not a very large hierarchy between the component, so there is no need to pass the server data down multiple levels to the desired query.

The second option might take more initial setup, but in the end, it makes the code base much simpler.

In the `pages/_app.tsx` file, we should wrap anything that is inside `QueryClientProvider` with `Hydrate`, as follows:

```
import { Hydrate, QueryClient, QueryClientProvider }
  from '@tanstack/react-query'

export const App = ({ Component, pageProps }) => {
  const [queryClient] = React.useState(() => new
    QueryClient())

  return (
    <QueryClientProvider client={queryClient}>
      <Hydrate state={pageProps.dehydratedState}>
        <Component {...pageProps} />
      </Hydrate>
    </QueryClientProvider>
  )
}
```

This will prepare the application to process any dehydrated state. But how do we provide a dehydrated state to the page?

On a specific page, we can modify `getStaticProps` or `getServerSideProps` as follows:

```
export const getServerSideProps = async () => {
    const queryClient = new QueryClient()

  await queryClient.prefetchQuery(['jobs'], getJobs)

  return {
    props: {
      dehydratedState: dehydrate(queryClient),
    },
  }
}
```

Then, we can consume the jobs as we would if we were fetching them on the client:

```
const JobsPage = () => {
    const jobs = useJobs();

    // ...
}
```

This will make it much easier to handle all the server states with React Query.

## Using query key factories

Having many queries all over the app might get pretty difficult to manage once the number of queries starts to grow. It is hard to track all the variations of the queries and where they are being used. Preventing duplicate query keys might be one of the problems as well.

That's why we should think about using query key factories instead of just deliberately adding the query keys all over the place.

We can define all potential keys in `src/lib/react-query.ts`:

First, we can define a simplified version of the factory:

```
const getQueryKeys = (baseKey: string) => {
  return {
```

```
    all: [baseKey],
    many: (params: Record<string, unknown>) => [baseKey,
      params],
    one: (id: string) => [baseKey, id],
  };
};
```

Then, we can create the keys for the queries:

```
export const queryKeys = {
  auth: {
    authUser: ['auth-user'],
  },
  jobs: getQueryKeys('jobs'),
  organizations: {
    one: getQueryKeys('organizations').one,
  },
};
```

As you can see, not all the features have the same key structure, but we can combine different factories to create what we need.

Then, if we wanted to use a key in a query, we could do so as follows:

```
const useJobs = () => {
    const { data, isLoading } = useQuery({
    queryKey: queryKeys.jobs.many(params),
    queryFn: () => getJobs({ params }),
    enabled: !!params.organizationId,
    initialData: [],
  });

  //...
}
```

What is good with this approach is that we have a centralized overview of all the keys, which reduces the possibility of making mistakes by mistyping a key or something similar.

This was an example of a simplified query key factory. If you need a more robust solution, there is a great library for this that can be found at https://www.npmjs.com/package/@lukemorales/query-key-factory.

## Code scaffolding

When looking at our application, we might notice that there is some level of boilerplate. Creating components, for example, requires a folder that looks like this:

```
- my-component
    - index.ts
    - my-component.tsx
```

We must remember to re-export the component from `index.ts` to make it available.

The same thing can be said for API requests. We need to create the request function and then the hook that consumes it. These things can be automated with tools that can help us generate these kinds of files easier via their CLI.

Having some scaffolding tools such as Plop.js and Hygen.io also brings better consistency to the code base.

## Validating form inputs and API responses with Zod

Let's talk briefly about validation. With validation, we want to make sure the data is in the expected form. For our application, we can validate form inputs and API responses.

For validation, we can use Zod, which is a great validation library that is TypeScript-first. This means that we can define a schema out of which we can infer types we can use.

### Form input validation

The `react-hooks-form` library comes with great support for Zod, which we could utilize for this. Taking the current login form, we could modify it so that it looks like this:

```
import { z } from 'zod';
import { yupResolver } from '@hookform/resolvers/yup';

const schema = z.object({
  email: z.string().min(1, 'Required'),
  password: z.string().min(1, 'Required'),
});
```

```
const LoginForm  = () => {
    const { register, handleSubmit } = useForm({
        resolver: yupResolver(schema);
    })

    // ...

    return (
        <Stack
      as="form"
      onSubmit={handleSubmit(onSubmit)}
      spacing="5"
      w="full"
  >
      <InputField
        label="Email"
        type="email"
        {...register('email')}
        error={formState.errors['email']}
      />
      <InputField
        label="Password"
        type="password"
        {...register('password')}
        error={formState.errors['password']}
      />
      <Button
        isLoading={login.isLoading}
        isDisabled={login.isLoading}
        type="submit"
      >
        Log in
      </Button>
    </Stack>
    )
}
```

Here, we are creating an object schema and providing that to `useForm` with the help of `yupResolver`.

This will make sure the form will never be submitted unless all the fields have valid values.

### API requests validation

We do have TypeScript types in place, but they don't protect us from runtime errors. That's why we should consider validating API responses in some cases. Let's take a look at the following example:

```
import { z } from 'zod';

const JobSchema = z.object({
    position: z.string(),
    info: z.string(),
    location: z.string()
});
```

Since Zod is a TypeScript-first library, we can use it to infer the types of the given object's shape:

```
type Job = z.infer<typeof JobSchema>
```

This might help with reducing duplicate type definitions. Finally, we can validate our requests, as follows:

```
const getJob = async () => {
    const jobResponse = await apiClient.get('/jobs/123');
    const job = JobSchema.parse(jobResponse);
    return job;
}
```

If any of the job properties do not match the schema, Zod will throw a runtime error, which we can then handle properly.

## Next.js 13

Next.js 13 is around the corner! It was released recently with some big changes, including the following:

- A new routing system with the app folder
- Server components
- A new data fetching approach

It's worth noting that it is backward compatible with older versions, so it allows incremental upgrades. It might take some time for everything to get polished out, but it is worth keeping an eye on it and upgrading to the new approach at some point.

# Appendix

There are a couple of topics that are not directly related to the application we built, but they are worth mentioning.

## GraphQL

Having a GraphQL API is a very common thing nowadays, especially in a microservices architecture. We worked with a REST API in our application, but how would we structure our API layer if it were a GraphQL API?

Well, the implementation would be very similar. We could choose to use a different library, such as Apollo, but we will stick with React Query.

Look at the following request:

```
import { request, gql } from "graphql-request";
import { useQuery } from '@tanstack/react-query';

const jobsQuery = gql`
    query {
        jobs {
            data {
                position
                department
                location
            }
        }
    }
`;

const getJobs = () => {
    return request('/api/graphql', jobsQuery);
};

const useJobs = () => {
```

```
const { data, isLoading } = useQuery({
    queryKey: ['jobs'],
    queryFn: getJobs
})

// ...
};
```

As you can see, first, we are defining the GraphQL query, which we then use to define the request function. Finally, we use the request function to create the useJobs hook.

## Monorepos

A **monorepo** is a Git repository that contains more than one project with a clearly defined relationship between those projects. This means that a good monorepo setup should provide the following features:

- Easy code sharing between projects
- Project constraints and visibility
- Computation caching
- Clear boundaries of the projects

It is worth exploring monorepos because they are being used in some of the largest software projects and make such large projects easier to manage.

Some of the most popular monorepo tools are as follows:

- Lerna
- Nx
- Turborepo
- Yarn workspaces

## Micro frontend architecture

**Micro frontend** architecture is a very interesting concept. It means that we can build and deploy components of the application as separate applications, and they would look and feel as if they were part of the same application.

Some of the benefits of using this kind of architecture are as follows:

- Useful when working on a platform that has many different teams.
- Does not constrain the apps to a specific technology. Each micro frontend application can have a different stack, and they would work together really well.

However, there are also some drawbacks:

- Building micro frontend architectures with different technologies, even though it's possible, should be discouraged. It is best to choose one framework and create standards for how the applications are built.
- Micro frontend architecture requires much more complex tooling, which for most of the use cases might not be worth it.

A couple of tools to explore are as follows:

- Module Federation
- Single SPA

## Summary

In this chapter, we went through the rest of the topics that are worth exploring after finishing this book. Things such as feature improvements and technical improvements can take your application to the next level. Hopefully, you can take what you have learned here and apply it to a similar real-world scenario.

# Index

# Other Books You May Enjoy

If you enjoyed this book, you may be interested in these other books by Packt:

**Micro State Management with React Hooks**

Daishi Kato

ISBN: 9781801812375

- Understand micro state management and how you can deal with global state.
- Build libraries using micro state management along with React Hooks.
- Discover how micro approaches are easy using React Hooks.
- Explore several approaches for implementing a global state.
- Understand the difference between component state and module state.

**Mastering React Test-Driven Development.**

Daniel Irvine

ISBN: 9781803247120

- Build test-driven applications using React 18 and Jest
- Understand techniques and patterns for writing great automated tests
- Use test doubles and mocks effectively
- Test-drive browser APIs, including the Fetch API and the WebSocket API
- Integrate with libraries such as React Router, Redux, and Relay (GraphQL)

## Packt is searching for authors like you

If you're interested in becoming an author for Packt, please visit `authors.packtpub.com` and apply today. We have worked with thousands of developers and tech professionals, just like you, to help them share their insight with the global tech community. You can make a general application, apply for a specific hot topic that we are recruiting an author for, or submit your own idea.

## Share Your Thoughts

Now you've finished *React Application Architecture for Production*, we'd love to hear your thoughts! Scan the QR code below to go straight to the Amazon review page for this book and share your feedback or leave a review on the site that you purchased it from.

`https://www.amazon.in/review/create-review/error?asin=1801070539`

Your review is important to us and the tech community and will help us make sure we're delivering excellent quality content.

# Download a free PDF copy of this book

Thanks for purchasing this book!

Do you like to read on the go but are unable to carry your print books everywhere?

Is your eBook purchase not compatible with the device of your choice?

Don't worry, now with every Packt book you get a DRM-free PDF version of that book at no cost.

Read anywhere, any place, on any device. Search, copy, and paste code from your favorite technical books directly into your application.

The perks don't stop there, you can get exclusive access to discounts, newsletters, and great free content in your inbox daily

Follow these simple steps to get the benefits:

1.  Scan the QR code or visit the link below

https://packt.link/free-ebook/9781801070539

2.  Submit your proof of purchase
3.  That's it! We'll send your free PDF and other benefits to your email directly

Made in the USA
Las Vegas, NV
20 May 2023

72327913R00129